Insight VCE Revision Questions

Legal Studies Units 3 & 4

First published in 2024
Insight Publications Pty Ltd
3/350 Charman Road
Cheltenham Victoria 3192
Australia
Tel: +61 3 8571 4950
Email: books@insightpublications.com.au

www.insightpublications.com.au

Insight VCE Revision Questions: Legal Studies Units 3 & 4

ISBN: 9781923154971

Written and reviewed by James Couzens and Mark Mitchell
Edited by Carole Lander
Cover by Melisa Paredes
Internal design and layout by Bec Yule @ Red Chilli Design

Printed by Markono Print Media Pte Ltd

Insight Publications acknowledges the Traditional Custodians of the Country on which we meet and work, the Boonwurrung People of the Kulin Nation. We pay our respects to their Elders past and present, and extend that respect to all Aboriginal and Torres Strait Islander peoples.

Contents

Introduction

This *VCE Revision Questions: Legal Studies Units 3 & 4* resource contains questions, suggested responses and tips to develop skills for assessment. We recommend using this resource as part of your study regime by completing sets of questions, as this process of applying your understanding and actively recalling information assists with deeper learning. You will also be able to review your answers and assess their appropriateness and correctness against the provided sample responses. Note that this resource complies with the 2024–2028 VCE Legal Studies Study Design.

The subject of Legal Studies encourages you to become an active and informed citizen by providing valuable insight into your relationship with the law and the legal system. You will develop knowledge and skills to enhance your confidence and ability to access and participate in the legal system. You will learn to appreciate the underlying principles of the rule of law and how legal systems and processes aim to achieve social cohesion, as well as how you can effect positive change to laws and the legal system.

By using *VCE Revision Questions: Legal Studies Units 3 & 4* as part of your study regime throughout the year, you will be prepared for questions you may encounter in your end-of-year VCE examination.

We wish you well with your studies.

The Insight Team

Questions

Unit 3 | Area of Study 1 The Victorian criminal justice system

Question 1 (4 marks)

Jane has been charged with murder. She intends to plead not guilty on the grounds of self-defence. If Jane is found guilty, she will face a sanction.

a. Define the term 'sanction'. 1 mark

b. Describe the sanction of imprisonment and outline **one** of its purposes. 3 marks

Question 2 (4 marks)

One right belonging to the accused is the right to trial by jury.

Describe **two** additional rights of the accused in the Victorian criminal justice system.

Question 3 (5 marks)

Ali has been charged with a summary offence and is required to attend a hearing at the Magistrates' Court of Victoria. Ali has only recently migrated to Australia; his income is limited, and his English skills are still developing. He is extremely worried about the forthcoming criminal proceeding, and he does not know where to turn.

Advise Ali about the options for legal assistance.

Question 4 (9 marks)

a. Plea negotiations serve multiple purposes within the criminal justice system.

Justify the existence of this process. 3 marks

b. Evaluate the capacity of **two** criminal sanctions to fulfil their respective purposes. 6 marks

Question 5 (11 marks)

Jill has been the victim of a serious assault. The assault occurred on a Friday evening when she was returning home from work. The episode left Jill physically and emotionally scarred. She found herself frequently fearing for her personal safety, both inside and outside her home. The perpetrator of the assault, Phillip, is a middle-aged homeless man with a history of drug addiction and mental health issues. A lawyer at the local community legal centre has advised Phillip to plead guilty. Phillip will plead guilty at the earliest opportunity. Sentencing will occur in the County Court.

a. Explain **one** right of the victim and **one** right of the defendant in this case. 4 marks

b. Explain **one** reason for the existence of a court hierarchy, making particular reference to this case. 3 marks

c. Discuss the appropriateness of the court considering mitigating circumstances and the early guilty plea in this case. 4 marks

Question 6 (15 marks)

Minh has been charged with multiple indictable offences. These offences relate to theft, burglary, armed robbery, assault and threat to kill. The victims of these offences, including the mother of two young children and an elderly man who lives alone, have been dramatically affected by the crimes. The mother has sought, and continues with, psychological counselling, and the elderly man is too terrified to leave the confines of his house and venture outside.

Despite the number of offences that Minh has been charged with, she is adamant that she is going to plead not guilty. She is worried about the potential outcome of the case because she has previously served a term of imprisonment for drug offences. During that term of imprisonment, she was unable to overcome her drug addiction and on one occasion she was severely beaten by a fellow inmate.

a. If Minh is found guilty of one or more of the charges that she is currently facing, the court will determine her sentence. A number of factors will be considered by the court when sentencing, including guilty pleas and victim impact statements.

Distinguish between these two factors and explain which will have a more substantial impact on the outcome of this case. 4 marks

b. Discuss the appropriateness of a plea negotiation in this case. 5 marks

c. Minh's lawyer has been giving much consideration to the potential outcomes of this case. She has decided that, if Minh is found guilty, she will push for a community corrections order at the sentencing hearing.

Discuss the ability of a community corrections order (CCO) to fulfil the purposes of criminal sanctions in Minh's case. 6 marks

Question 7 (16 marks)

Source 1

The following excerpt is from a document produced by the Department of Justice and Community Safety.

> Prior reforms to the criminal justice process have improved the early management of cases in the criminal justice system. The reduction of delay in criminal cases improves efficiency and reduces the risk of trauma and stress experienced by witnesses and victims. Minimising the number of times a witness is required to give evidence, increasing available protections for vulnerable witnesses when giving evidence, and appropriately managing questioning of witnesses also serve to better protect witnesses from stress and trauma in the criminal trial process.
>
> Despite these improvements, there are still significant delays in criminal proceedings and there is scope for further reform to improve the experience of witnesses in the criminal justice system. As part of a number of other initiatives, the release of this discussion paper is an opportunity to make further changes to address delay and improve the experience of witnesses in the criminal justice system.

Source: <https://engage.vic.gov.au/reducing-trauma-and-delay-for-witnesses-and-victims>
© State of Victoria (Department of Premier and Cabinet) 2016.

Source 2

The following excerpt is adapted from the Supreme Court of Victoria's 2020–2025 strategic statement.

> Our goal and purpose are underpinned by the following values: …
>
> Ensuring … equal protection of the law to all those before the Court, including in criminal cases …
>
> Enabling simple entry to the legal process; ensuring cases are managed and determined fairly. Ensuring that the Court's processes are clear, consistent, user-friendly and non-discriminatory. Making the Court physically available to all …
>
> Maintaining systems and supports to ensure the integrity of the Court and its work. Conducting our hearings in public and making them available for viewing through technological means where appropriate …
>
> Striving to perform all of our functions efficiently and disposing of cases within an appropriate time. Aiming to deliver judgments within a reasonable time …
>
> Writing judgments that are clear, concise and easy to understand …
>
> Being a leader in innovation and embracing changes in technology and court processes, while still respecting traditions that continue to serve the Court and the community well …
>
> Treating all Court users with courtesy and respect. Respecting and promoting diversity.

Source: adapted excerpt from the Supreme Court of Victoria's 2020–2025 Strategic Statement. <https://www.supremecourt.vic.gov.au/about-the-court/strategic-statement>

Source 3

The following excerpt is adapted from the website of the Commonwealth Attorney-General's Department.

> **What are minimum guarantees in criminal proceedings?**
>
> Minimum guarantees in criminal proceedings include:
>
> - to be informed promptly of the charge
> - to have adequate time and facilities to prepare a defence and to communicate with counsel
> - to be tried without undue delay
> - to be tried in person
> - to have legal assistance assigned to the accused, where the interests of justice so require, and without payment if the accused is unable to pay for it
> - to cross-examine prosecution witnesses and to obtain the attendance and examination of witnesses on behalf of the accused on the same conditions as the prosecution
> - to have the assistance of an interpreter
> - to have a conviction and sentence reviewed by a higher court

Source: <https://www.ag.gov.au/RightsAndProtections/HumanRights/Human-rights-scrutiny/PublicSectorGuidanceSheets/Pages/Minimumguaranteesincriminalproceedings.aspx> © Commonwealth of Australia 2019.

a. Outline **two** factors that affect the ability of the criminal justice system to achieve the principles of justice. 4 marks

b. Explain how the Supreme Court of Victoria aims to fulfil the principles of justice between 2020 and 2025. 6 marks

c. With reference to the key personnel within a criminal case, explain how the rights of the accused are protected. 6 marks

Question 8 (3 marks)

Johnny was recently arrested and charged with murder and attempted murder. He had hosted a barbecue at his family property to which he had invited five guests. Police alleged the main meal, marinated chicken wings, led to four guests being poisoned. Three of the guests died. One of the guests, having been in a coma in hospital, survived.

Explain whether the case involved summary offences or indictable offences.

Question 9 (3 marks)

Explain how the presumption of innocence is protected within the criminal justice system.

Question 10 (3 marks)

The right to silence is one right belonging to an accused within the criminal justice system. Describe the relationship between the right to silence and the principle of fairness.

Question 11 (14 marks)

In September 2022, a jury presiding over a rape case, involving accused offender Frank, was discharged. It had been found that a particular juror had accessed information which had not been presented as evidence in court. During the trial, the accuser, Amaya, took the stand and spent several days in the witness box. The accused did not give evidence.

a. Outline how the standard of proof in the above matter relates to fairness. 2 marks

b. With reference to the burden of proof, explain why there was no need for the accused to take the stand in this matter. 3 marks

c. Analyse the role of the jury in this case. 5 marks

d. Explain how either Victoria Legal Aid or a community legal centre could have assisted the victim in this case. 4 marks

Question 12 (6 marks)

Discuss how cultural differences can affect the achievement of the principles of justice within the criminal justice system.

Unit 3 | Area of Study 2 The Victorian civil justice system

Question 1 (5 marks)

Despite not being overly wealthy, John has a passion for collectables. When he purchased two movie posters, he decided to have them framed. While completing their work, the framers damaged one of the posters. In John's opinion, the overall quality of the framing job was questionable as well. In total, the framing work cost $500. John attempted to enter into negotiation with the framers in order to get his money back but they refused to get involved in the discussion. John's friend suggested that he take the matter to the Victorian Civil and Administrative Tribunal (VCAT).

Advise John about whether VCAT is the most appropriate body to help him resolve this dispute. Provide **three** distinct arguments in your advice to John.

Question 2 (3 marks)

Sheena wishes to sue Adriano. Adriano does not feel that he has infringed Sheena's rights. The upcoming trial in the Supreme Court Trial Division is expected to last a number of weeks. Despite the fact that Sheena believes her rights have been infringed, her lawyer has encouraged her to consider settling the matter out of court.

Explain **one** factor that Sheena might have considered when she initiated civil action.

Question 3 (8 marks)

Sarah is not satisfied with the work of a building company that she employed to renovate her house. She firmly believes that the work is of poor quality and that some of the agreements reached prior to the commencement of renovations have not been fulfilled. Sarah is aware of the challenges associated with initiating legal action, but she is willing to pursue the matter in court if necessary.

a. Describe **one** method that Sarah could use to resolve the matter that will not require her appearance in court. 2 marks

b. Sarah will need to consider a number of factors prior to initiating a civil claim in court. One factor is the limitation of actions. Another factor is enforcement issues.

Analyse these two factors. 3 marks

c. Consider the possible civil remedies Sarah could pursue in this case.

To what extent would **one** remedy fulfil its purpose in this instance? 3 marks

Question 4 (2 marks)

Outline **one** responsibility of a judge in a civil trial.

Question 5 (9 marks)

In the course of Yashiro's employment transporting goods by truck, he was involved in a significant accident. Yashiro had been working long hours and was deprived of sleep. He had been taking an excessive amount of medication in an attempt to handle the demands of his job. On the evening in question, Yashiro failed to see a stop signal and crashed into another car at a busy intersection. The other driver, Sharon, was badly injured in the crash. Sharon missed many months of work and also required multiple operations. Despite these operations, she is likely to experience ongoing pain and discomfort for the rest of her life. Sharon decided to initiate civil action.

a. Identify the party with whom the burden of proof lies in this case and explain what the standard of proof in a civil matter entails. 3 marks

b. Describe the civil remedies of damages and injunctions and discuss the ability of possible civil remedies to fulfil their purposes in this case. 6 marks

Question 6 (3 marks)

One day, Jo, an inmate who had been imprisoned for fraud, tripped on a prison step in need of repair, badly injuring her back. This injury continues to cause Jo considerable pain, and she has been unable to work since her release from prison. Jo has been intending to sue the state as a result of the grievances stemming from her term of imprisonment.

Identify which party possesses the burden of proof and outline the standard of proof if Jo proceeds to launch civil action.

Question 7 (10 marks)

In 2021, details of a report into cultural safety at a local sporting club were revealed in the media. Specifically, a number of BIPOC (Black, Indigenous, people of colour) players who had been involved with the club had spoken of their mistreatment. It was hoped that mediation between club figures accused of wrongdoing and former BIPOC players would take place.

a. Discuss the appropriateness of mediation in this matter. 6 marks

b. Justify why the infringed parties might have benefited from using a court to resolve this dispute. 4 marks

Question 8 (4 marks)

Justify the existence of a court hierarchy within the civil justice system.

Question 9 (19 marks)

In November 2020, a state fishing club was found liable by a Supreme Court jury in a negligence case initiated by Luc. Luc worked with the club when he was a young boy and at that time he was abused by a volunteer called Tank. In court, it was ruled that the club had failed in its duty to protect Luc. At the end of the three-week trial, the jury awarded Luc $3 million for pain and suffering, $2.6 million for loss of earnings, and $87 000 for medical costs.

a. Describe the roles of the parties in this case. 6 marks

b. Compare the role of a criminal jury with that of a civil jury. 4 marks

c. Suggest what would have made a class action appropriate in this case. 4 marks

d. Explain why legal practitioners are necessary in a case such as this one. 5 marks

Question 10 (6 marks)

The following information is available on the Consumer Affairs Victoria website.

> If you have tried to resolve your problem or complaint yourself and it remains unresolved, we may choose to offer assistance through our voluntary dispute services.
>
> We accept complaints in the following circumstances:
>
> - The problem is about a business or rental provider/property manager. We do not accept complaints about consumers or renters.
> - You have made a reasonable attempt to resolve the problem with the business or rental provider/property manager.
> - The problem is within our jurisdiction and not more appropriately handled by another organisation.
> - Legislation or contractual rights appear to have been breached.
> - The problem has a reasonable chance of being resolved.
> - You have paid by credit card and a chargeback has failed to resolve the problem.
> - The courts or a tribunal have not already ruled on the matter, and there is no case pending.
>
> If we decide your problem is suitable for our dispute services, we will:
>
> - contact the business or rental provider/property manager on your behalf
> - identify the issues
> - explore options for a resolution that are consistent with the law.
>
> We cannot make anyone speak to us and we cannot enforce an outcome – only a court or tribunal have this power. If our involvement does not resolve the problem, we will generally give you information on taking your complaint further by applying to a court or tribunal, such as the Victorian Civil and Administrative Tribunal (VCAT), or getting your own legal advice.

Source: <https://www.consumer.vic.gov.au/contact-us/resolve-your-problem>
© State of Victoria (Consumer Affairs Victoria) 2023

Discuss the appropriateness of the involvement of Consumer Affairs Victoria in the resolution of civil disputes.

Question 11 (10 marks)

With reference to the impact of costs and time, evaluate the ability of the civil justice system to achieve the principles of justice.

Question 12 (10 marks)

Discuss the extent to which the defendant in both criminal and civil matters has the ability to access the justice system.

Unit 4 | Area of Study 1 The people and the law-makers

Question 1 (4 marks)

Explain the significance of **one** High Court case that has had an impact on the division of constitutional law-making powers.

Question 2 (6 marks)

Evaluate the extent to which the express protection of rights acts as a check on parliament in law-making.

Question 3 (5 marks)

In the High Court case of *British American Tobacco Australasia Limited & Ors v Commonwealth of Australia*, the plaintiffs questioned the validity of the *Tobacco Plain Packaging Act 2011* (Cth), which was to regulate and standardise the retail packaging and appearance of tobacco products in Australia. The High Court held that the law was constitutional, confirming the powers of the Commonwealth to pass such law.

Explain the significance of **one** other High Court case that has had an impact on the division of law-making powers.

Question 4 (4 marks)

Source 1

The following is an extract from the Victorian Law Reform Commission's website.

> In December 2014, the Attorney-General asked the Commission to review the law to allow people to be treated with medicinal cannabis in exceptional circumstances.
>
> The Commission's March 2015 issues paper identified two areas of investigation:
>
> - How to define the exceptional circumstances in which a person should be allowed to use medicinal cannabis
> - How the law could be amended to enable patients to obtain medicinal cannabis while continuing to prevent unauthorised access.
>
> Our subsequent investigation drew on nine public consultations in metropolitan and regional Victoria and 99 public submissions.
>
> The final report on medicinal cannabis law reform was delivered to the Attorney-General on 31 August 2015. The report made 42 recommendations for changes to the law to allow people to be treated with medicinal cannabis in exceptional circumstances. The report was tabled in Parliament on 6 October 2015 …

Source: Victorian Law Reform Commission website,
<https://www.lawreform.vic.gov.au/all-projects/medicinal-cannabis>

Source 2

The following is an extract from the Parliament of Victoria's website.

> On 8 December 2015, the Andrews Government introduced the *Access to Medicinal Cannabis Bill 2015* to the Legislative Assembly, thereby becoming the first Australian government to introduce a Bill to legalise medicinal cannabis through establishing a state-based medicinal cannabis scheme. The Bill provides for cultivation, manufacture and distribution of medicinal cannabis products in Victoria.
>
> The Bill follows a pre-election commitment in August 2014 by the then Opposition Leader Daniel Andrews to pursue legalisation of medicinal cannabis. After the state election in November 2014, the Andrews Government asked the Victorian Law Reform Commission (VLRC) to review law reform options to enable access to medicinal cannabis for patients in exceptional circumstances. This Bill responds to recommendations in the VLRC's report.

Source: Parliament of Victoria website,
<https://www.parliament.vic.gov.au/component/jdownloads/download/36-research-papers/13760-2016-2-access-to-medicinal-cannabis-bill2015>

Source 3

The following is an excerpt from the *Access to Medicinal Cannabis Act 2016* (Vic).

> ***eligible patient*** means—
>
> a. a patient who—
>
> (i) is under 18 years of age; and
>
> (i) experiences severe seizures resulting from an epileptic condition in respect of which other treatment options have not proved effective or have generated intolerable side effects; and
>
> (i) meets the prescribed criteria in respect of that condition (if any); or
>
> b. a patient who—
>
> (i) has a prescribed medical condition; and
>
> (ii) meets the prescribed criteria in respect of that condition (if any);

Source: Victorian Legislation and Parliamentary Documents website,

<http://www.legislation.vic.gov.au/Domino/Web_Notes/LDMS/PubStatbook.nsf/edfb620cf7503d1aca256da4001b08af/1E1D95ECB3B1662ECA257FA100098BF7/$FILE/16-020aa%20authorised.pdf>

With reference to the division of constitutional law-making powers, explain how the Victorian Parliament is able to make law to allow access to medicinal cannabis.

Question 5 (9 marks)

The following is an excerpt from the National Party of Australia's website.

> **Keeping Australians safe is the Morrison Government's first priority.**
>
> The online world brings with it the ability to connect with people all over the world as never before. But with these opportunities come new threats and challenges. The Morrison Government is committed to a safer online environment for all Australians, including families and children. The online world is no longer an optional extra in people's lives. The online world should not be an ungoverned space. The targets of online abuse and bullying should not be forced offline. Instead, technology platforms, governments and other users must all play a part in making the internet safe. It is why we have taken action to crack down on online predators as well as giving parents and carers the information and support they need to ensure their children's safety in the online world. We understand that Australians expect the laws and standards of behaviour that apply in the physical world should apply equally in the online world.

Source: National Party of Australia © National Party of Australia <https://nationals.org.au/our-plan-to-keep-australians-safe-online/>

a. With reference to the Crown and the Houses of Parliament, outline what would be required when the government proposes laws to protect the 'targets of online abuse and bullying'. 6 marks

b. Explain what could happen if the state of Victoria made law that conflicted with the Commonwealth's efforts to regulate the 'online world'. 3 marks

Question 6 (3 marks)

Explain how judicial activism **or** judicial conservatism can affect the ability of courts to make law.

Question 7 (8 marks)

Discuss **two** factors that affect the ability of parliament to make law.

Question 8 (4 marks)

As at 14 November 2019, the composition of the Senate of the Commonwealth Parliament was as follows.

- 35 members of the Liberal–National Coalition
- 26 members of the Australian Labor Party
- 9 members of the Australian Greens
- 2 members of the Centre Alliance
- 2 members of Pauline Hanson's One Nation Party
- 1 member of the Jacqui Lambie Network
- 1 independent

Discuss the extent to which the Senate is representative in its law-making.

Question 9 (10 marks)

In 1996 Sir Anthony Mason, a renowned judge of the High Court, addressed the issue of courts as law-makers:

> I had learned that judges do make law some 25 years before Lord Reid [one of England's greatest judges] made his public statement [on the issue] in 1972. Of course, some judges had acknowledged as much before 1972. Viscount Radcliffe, another great English judge, had said as much in 1967, but he cautioned against letting the public in on the secret lest it harm public confidence in the law 'as a constant, safe in the hands of judges'.

Discuss the extent to which judges are able to make law in Australian courts.

Question 10 (3 marks)

The following is an extract from the Parliament of Victoria website, updated in 2018.

Terms of Reference

On 11 November 2015, the Legislative Council issues the attached terms of reference for the Inquiry into Illicit and Synthetic Drugs and Prescription Medication.

The Law Reform, Road and Community Safety Committee has since refined the terms of reference and amended the inquiry title to the Inquiry into Drug Law Reform.

The Committee will inquire into, consider and report, no later than 29 March 2018 on:

1) The effectiveness of laws, procedures and regulations relating to illicit and synthetic drugs and the misuse of prescription medication in minimising drug-related health, social and economic harm; and
2) The practice of other Australian states and territories and overseas jurisdictions and their approach to drug law reform and how other positive reforms could be adopted into Victorian law.

Source: Parliament of Victoria website,
<https://www.parliament.vic.gov.au/lrrcsc/inquiries/article/2809>
© Parliament of Victoria 2018

The *Access to Medicinal Cannabis Act 2016* (Vic) refers to an 'eligible patient' in relation to those who can access medicinal cannabis.

In the future, a court may be required to interpret the term 'eligible patient'.

Explain **one** impact of this interpretation. 3 marks

Question 11 (10 marks)

The High Court of Australia case of *State Government Insurance Commission v Trigwell* (1979) was significant. The Trigwell family were injured in a collision between their vehicle and another car. The other driver (who died in the accident) had lost control of their vehicle due to roaming livestock. The Trigwells sought compensation from the deceased negligent driver's insurance company and the owner of the livestock.

An old precedent was applied, which outlined that the owner of roaming livestock could not be held liable for damage caused by the animals. As a result of the precedent, the owner of the roaming livestock did not have to pay damages to the injured family (the Trigwells), but the insurance company did.

The State Government Insurance Commission appealed to the High Court, believing the original decision to be unjust and hoping that the High Court would change the law. However, the original decision was upheld, as the majority of High Court justices believed the old precedent was still applicable. These High Court justices did not embrace the role of law-maker.

Subsequent to this High Court decision, the Parliament of Victoria passed a law abrogating the old precedent. As a result, farmers would now be held liable for damage caused by their roaming livestock.

a. Explain **two** factors that affected the ability of the High Court to change the law in this case. 4 marks

b. 'Parliament and the courts are totally separate and distinct institutions. There is no connection between them in any way when it comes to law-making.'

Discuss the accuracy of the above statement, making reference to the case of *State Government Insurance Commission v Trigwell.* 6 marks

Question 12 (2 marks)

Outline the role of the Crown in law-making at Commonwealth level.

Question 13 (4 marks)

Distinguish between the role of the upper house and the lower house of the Parliament of Victoria.

Question 14 (5 marks)

Explain how the separation of the legislative, executive and judicial powers acts as a check on parliament in law-making.

Question 15 (5 marks)

Explain how the High Court has protected the principle of representative government.

Question 16 (4 marks)

Mansfield v Kelly (1972) saw the Full Court of the Supreme Court – now known as the Supreme Court (Court of Appeal) – interpreting words within the *Summary Offences Act 1966* (Vic). The court needed to determine whether the defendant was guilty of being drunk in a public place. The defendant had been found in an intoxicated state in the front seat of a motor car parked on a public street. The court held that a person found drunk in a motor car that is in a public street is 'found drunk in a public place'.

Source: Summary Offences Act 1966 and Victorian Reports
<https://victorianreports.com.au/judgment/view/1972-VR-744>

Outline **two** effects of the court's interpretation of legislation in this case.

Unit 4 | Area of Study 2 The people and reform

Question 1 (4 marks)

In recent years, there have been a number of parliamentary committees and royal commissions at both state and federal government levels.

In late 2019, the Parliament of Victoria website referred to 'the Integrity and Oversight Committee … a joint investigatory committee of the Parliament of Victoria … created when the Accountability and Oversight Committee and the Independent Broad-based Anti-corruption Commission Committee were amalgamated'.

Source: Parliament of Victoria website <https://web.archive.org/web/20220320111312/https://www.parliament.vic.gov.au/ioc> © Parliament of Victoria 2019

At the same time, the ABC reported the following on the Royal Commission into the Management of Police Informants: 'Former Victoria Police Chief Commissioner Christine Nixon has told the Lawyer X royal commission she was never told that [gangland lawyer] Nicola Gobbo was a police informer …'

Source: 'Former police chief Christine Nixon tells Lawyer X royal commission she was never told of Nicola Gobbo's role' by Sarah Farnsworth and staff, ABC News <https://www.abc.net.au/news/2019-12-18/carl-williams-killing-involved-corrupt-prison-staff-ken-jones/11808880>

Explain the role of royal commissions **or** parliamentary committees in law reform.

Question 2 (17 marks)

Source 1

The following is an extract from the Royal Commission into Family Violence website.

In keeping with its terms of reference, the Royal Commission into Family Violence aimed to make recommendations which [among other things]:

- foster a violence-free society
- reduce and aim to eliminate family violence
- prevent the occurrence and escalation of family violence
- build respectful family relationships …
- support adults and children who have been affected by family violence
- hold those who have been violent accountable for their actions
- help people who use or may use family violence to change their behaviour.

Source: Royal Commission into Family Violence website, <www.rcfv.com.au/The-Commission>

Source 2

The following is an extract from the Victoria Legal Aid website.

Our submission to the Royal Commission

Our submission to the Royal Commission into Family Violence made 35 recommendations to improve the legal response to family violence …

We support a system that:

- recognises the unique preventative role and value of family violence legal services for both applicants and respondents
- improves the operational processes supporting the legal response to family violence
- promotes rehabilitation where appropriate once a criminal justice response is triggered by responding to the individual circumstances of people who commit criminal offences in the context of family violence.

Source: Victoria Legal Aid website, <www.legalaid.vic.gov.au/about-us/strategic-advocacy-and-law-reform/more-effective-responses-to-family-violence/royal-commission-into-family-violence>

Source 3

The following is an extract from the Parliament of Victoria website, updated in 2018.

> **Terms of Reference**
>
> On 11 November 2015, the Legislative Council issues the attached terms of reference for the Inquiry into Illicit and Synthetic Drugs and Prescription Medication.
>
> The Law Reform, Road and Community Safety Committee has since refined the terms of reference and amended the inquiry title to the Inquiry into Drug Law Reform.
>
> The Committee will inquire into, consider and report, no later than 29 March 2018 on:
>
> (3) The effectiveness of laws, procedures and regulations relating to illicit and synthetic drugs and the misuse of prescription medication in minimising drug-related health, social and economic harm; and
>
> (4) The practice of other Australian states and territories and overseas jurisdictions and their approach to drug law reform and how other positive reforms could be adopted into Victorian law.

Source: Parliament of Victoria website,
<https://www.parliament.vic.gov.au/lrrcsc/inquiries/article/2809>

a. Explain **one** way in which the terms of reference and aims of **either** the Royal Commission into Family Violence **or** the Law Reform, Road and Community Safety Committee's Inquiry into Drug Law Reform restrict the selected body from influencing change in the law. 3 marks

b. Evaluate the individual's ability and means to influence law reform.
In your answer, refer to **either** royal commissions **or** parliamentary committees and at least one of the following: petitions; demonstrations; the use of courts. 6 marks

c. 'While royal commissions and parliamentary committees can influence law reform, one should not forget the vital role played by the Victorian Law Reform Commission (VLRC).'

With reference to the VLRC, discuss the extent to which you agree with this statement. 8 marks

Question 3 (6 marks)

Source 1

The following is an extract from the Victorian Law Reform Commission (VLRC)'s website.

> In December 2014, the Attorney-General asked the Commission to review the law to allow people to be treated with medicinal cannabis in exceptional circumstances.
>
> The Commission's March 2015 issues paper identified two areas of investigation:
>
> - How to define the exceptional circumstances in which a person should be allowed to use medicinal cannabis
> - How the law could be amended to enable patients to obtain medicinal cannabis while continuing to prevent unauthorised access.
>
> Our subsequent investigation drew on nine public consultations in metropolitan and regional Victoria and 99 public submissions.
>
> The final report on medicinal cannabis law reform was delivered to the Attorney-General on 31 August 2015. The report made 42 recommendations for changes to the law to allow people to be treated with medicinal cannabis in exceptional circumstances. The report was tabled in Parliament on 6 October 2015 …

Source: Victorian Law Reform Commission website,
<https://www.lawreform.vic.gov.au/all-projects/medicinal-cannabis>

Source 2

The following is an extract from the Parliament of Victoria's website.

> On 8 December 2015, the Andrews Government introduced the *Access to Medicinal Cannabis Bill 2015* to the Legislative Assembly, thereby becoming the first Australian government to introduce a Bill to legalise medicinal cannabis through establishing a state-based medicinal cannabis scheme. The Bill provides for cultivation, manufacture and distribution of medicinal cannabis products in Victoria.
>
> The Bill follows a pre-election commitment in August 2014 by the then Opposition Leader Daniel Andrews to pursue legalisation of medicinal cannabis. After the state election in November 2014, the Andrews Government asked the Victorian Law Reform Commission (VLRC) to review law reform options to enable access to medicinal cannabis for patients in exceptional circumstances. This Bill responds to recommendations in the VLRC's report.

Source: Parliament of Victoria website,
https://www.parliament.vic.gov.au/component/jdownloads/download/36-research-papers/13760-2016-2-access-to-medicinal-cannabis-bill2015

a. With reference to introducing access to medicinal cannabis, outline **one** reason for law reform. 2 marks

b. Evaluate the ability of the VLRC to influence law reform regarding access to medicinal cannabis. 4 marks

Question 4 (9 marks)

The following is an excerpt from the National Party of Australia's website.

> **Keeping Australians safe is the Morrison Government's first priority.**
>
> The online world brings with it the ability to connect with people all over the world as never before. But with these opportunities come new threats and challenges.
>
> The Morrison Government is committed to a safer online environment for all Australians, including families and children.
>
> The online world is no longer an optional extra in people's lives. The online world should not be an ungoverned space. The targets of online abuse and bullying should not be forced offline. Instead, technology platforms, governments and other users must all play a part in making the internet safe.
>
> It is why we have taken action to crack down on online predators as well as giving parents and carers the information and support they need to ensure their children's safety in the online world.
>
> We understand that Australians expect the laws and standards of behaviour that apply in the physical world should apply equally in the online world.

Source: National Party of Australia © National Party of Australia
https://nationals.org.au/our-plan-to-keep-australians-safe-online/

a. Identify **one** reason why there is a need to change the law. 3 marks

b. In your view, what would be the **two** most effective methods for individuals to influence law-makers? Give reasons for your answer. 6 marks

Question 5 (4 marks)

With use of examples, analyse the role of the media, including social media, in law reform.

Question 6 (8 marks)

With reference to one recent example relating to the civil or criminal justice system, evaluate the ability of the Victorian Law Reform Commission to influence change in the law.

Question 7 (3 marks)

Outline **one** reason for constitutional reform.

Question 8 (6 marks)

With reference to the 1967 referendum, explain how the written words of the Australian Constitution can be changed.

Question 9 (4 marks)

Suggest **two** reasons why a referendum might fail.

Question 10 (10 marks)

'Despite the many ways individuals can influence law reform, including social media, parliament and the courts are limited in their ability to respond to the need for law reform.'

Discuss the extent to which you agree with this statement. In your answer, provide **one** reason for law reform.

Suggested responses

Unit 3 | Area of Study 1 The Victorian criminal justice system

Question 1a

Sample response

A sanction is the consequence handed down by a court when an individual pleads guilty to, or is found guilty of, a criminal charge.

Mark allocation: 1 mark

- 1 mark for correctly defining the term 'sanction'.

TIP

» **Provide a precise and accurate definition. You should not spend too long or go into too much detail when answering questions that are only worth one mark.**

Question 1b

Sample response

The sanction of imprisonment is the most serious of all criminal sanctions. It is imposed in cases of significant criminal behaviour and is viewed as a last resort. Imprisonment involves depriving the offender of their liberty and the removal of certain rights and privileges. If an offender is found guilty of multiple charges, and given multiple terms of imprisonment, those terms might be served cumulatively or concurrently. If served cumulatively, they will be served one after another. If served concurrently, the sentences will be served at the same time. An offender who receives a sentence of more than two years' imprisonment must have a non-parole period set by the court.

One purpose of imprisonment is to deter. Specific deterrence focuses on discouraging the offender from future criminal activity; general deterrence focuses on discouraging society as a whole from engaging in criminal activity.

Mark allocation: 3 marks

- 2 marks for a description of imprisonment.
- 1 mark for outlining one of the purposes of imprisonment.

Note: Responses may also mention the fact that prison terms are expressed in levels. There are nine levels, with Level 1 equating to life imprisonment, Level 2 equating to 25 years' imprisonment and Level 9 equating to 6 months' imprisonment.

Question 2

Sample response

One further right belonging to the accused is the right to be tried without unreasonable delay. Section 25 of the Victorian Charter of Human Rights and Responsibilities provides for many rights in criminal proceedings, with one such right being the right of the accused to be tried without unreasonable delay. To protect the rights of the accused and to achieve the principles of justice, court proceedings must be held within a reasonable amount of time after a charge is made. Of course, time must be allowed for an allegation to be fully investigated and for a court to hear all relevant evidence. However, it is also important that criminal cases should not be unduly delayed.

Another right belonging to the accused is the right to silence. When being questioned by the police, the accused does not have to respond, although they must provide their name and address. The right to silence ensures an accused does not incriminate himself or herself, resulting in fairness. No adverse inferences can be drawn by a jury if an accused chooses to retain the right to silence. In addition, no adverse inferences can be drawn if the accused chooses not to take the stand or if the accused does not mount a defence.

Mark allocation: 4 marks

- 1 mark for accurately identifying each additional right (up to 2 marks).
- 1 mark for describing what each right entails (up to 2 marks).

Question 3

Sample response

Ali has a number of options for seeking legal assistance, particularly given his disadvantaged state. First, he could make contact with Victoria Legal Aid (VLA). VLA is a government-funded body that aims to provide equal access to the legal system for all Victorians, regardless of their circumstances, offering them free legal information and education. There are 15 VLA offices in Victoria and appointments can be made to see a lawyer for free legal advice. A telephone hotline exists, as does a website. Funding for legal representation can also be provided. In order to gain legal representation in a criminal matter, the accused must meet strict eligibility criteria, including consideration of the benefit to the public and the accused's financial position. Any of these services would benefit Ali.

Secondly, Ali could approach a community legal centre (CLC), which exists to provide free legal advice and information. CLCs are independent bodies focusing on disadvantaged groups and people with special needs. Ali would fit into this category. There are 24 CLCs that provide general legal support and a number of additional specialist CLCs. In relation to providing ongoing legal support, certain eligibility requirements need to be met. The accused's personal circumstances and financial position will be considered. An example of a CLC is the Ballarat and Grampians Community Legal Service.

Mark allocation: 5 marks

- 1 mark for identifying VLA.
- 1 mark for identifying CLCs.
- 3 marks for explaining in detail how VLA and CLCs can specifically help Ali.

TIP

» **Given that the question asks for 'options' (plural), you must discuss both Victoria Legal Aid and community legal centres.**

Question 4a

Sample response

> Plea negotiations serve many vital purposes within the criminal justice system, significantly enhancing its efficiency.
>
> If a plea negotiation is successfully undertaken, trial will be avoided. As a result of trial being avoided, the state and the accused will save time and money. Time and money will be saved as there will be no need to employ legal representation for an extended period; there will be no need to prepare and present a case for trial; there will be no need to utilise court personnel for this particular matter. In addition, the burden on the legal system will be reduced, enhancing access; contested matters will be able to proceed to trial more rapidly.
>
> A further benefit of plea negotiation is that witnesses will not have to provide evidence at trial. Providing oral testimony can be enormously traumatic, resulting in secondary victimisation; such trauma will be avoided if an accused decides to plead guilty to a lesser charge or a reduced number of charges.
>
> Finally, plea negotiations guarantee a conviction. If the prosecution is concerned about the strength of its evidence, it might prefer to engage in discussions that will result in the accused being convicted.

Mark allocation: 3 marks

- 1 mark for each justification for a plea negotiation.

TIP

» **When required to justify, you must provide reasons or benefits associated with an action or procedure.**

Question 4b

Sample response

> One criminal sanction that fulfils several purposes is imprisonment. Imprisonment, the harshest sanction, serves to punish the offender. This is achieved by restricting the offender's liberty and removing certain rights. In addition, imprisonment serves to protect society. Protection stems from the removal of the offender from society. Also, imprisonment fulfils the purpose of denunciation. The imposing of this most serious of sanctions makes the court's disapproval of the offender, and his or her actions, clear.
>
> However, imprisonment does not effectively address all purposes of sanctions. It is difficult to successfully rehabilitate an inmate. While certain programs, such as education and drug programs, do exist within jails, the environment of a prison and what imprisonment entails can make improving oneself difficult. The ability of imprisonment to deter offending must also be questioned. Given more than 60% of Australia's prison population has previously been incarcerated, it appears many are not discouraged from committing further crimes.
>
> Another sanction that fulfils a number of purposes is a community correction order (CCO). A CCO can achieve the aim of punishment. It does this by placing restrictions on the movement of offenders, such as not being able to leave Victoria without permission. An offender might also be required to complete up to 600 hours of unpaid community work. In addition, a CCO can rehabilitate offenders. Conditions requiring programs, such as counselling, can be attached to such orders. Advocates argue protection can be achieved because an offender might be restricted from associating with certain individuals or frequenting certain places through additional conditions.
>
> However, questions as to the effectiveness of community corrections orders can be raised. Some will see them as a 'soft' option. Therefore, they might not act to sufficiently punish or denounce the offender. In relation to the former, the individual remains in society and, in terms of the latter, the individual remains in society and their actions might not receive sufficient criticism. Critics could also ask whether a CCO adequately deters the specific individual and broader society from offending, given the offender is not incarcerated and retains multiple freedoms.

Mark allocation: 6 marks

- 3 marks for an evaluation of one sanction.
- 3 marks for an evaluation of a second sanction.

TIP

» **When evaluating a sanction, you must address how a sanction might fulfil the purposes of sanctions, and also how a sanction might not fulfil the purposes of sanctions.**

Question 5a

Sample response

Both the victim and the defendant will have certain rights in this matter.

If Phillip was to change his plea from guilty to not guilty, the victim, Jill, would have the right to give evidence using alternative arrangements. A witness requiring alternative arrangements could be a child or a person with a cognitive impairment, the victim of a violent offence, including domestic violence, or the victim of a sexual offence. Special provisions will be put in place if providing testimony at trial would present particular difficulties or have certain consequences for the victim. Special provisions might include having a friend or relative in court while evidence is given, provided the support person is not appearing as a witness; having a screen in the court, so that the witness does not have to see the accused while giving evidence; providing testimony through CCTV; and having the court closed to the public while evidence is given. Jill, who was left physically and emotionally scarred from the serious assault, would benefit from such provisions.

The defendant, Phillip, will have the right to be tried without unreasonable delay. Section 25 of the Victorian Charter of Human Rights and Responsibilities provides for many rights in criminal proceedings and one of them is the right to be tried without unreasonable delay. Court proceedings must be held within a reasonable amount of time after a charge is made. Time must be allowed for an allegation to be fully investigated and for a court to hear all relevant evidence. If Phillip maintains his stance to plead guilty, a trial will be avoided, and sentencing will occur relatively rapidly.

Note: Additional rights of the victim that could be addressed are provided below.

- The victim will have the right to be informed of the offender's likely release date. If the victim applies to be placed on the Victims Register, they can gain information about the offender. The victim can be provided with information about an offender who was imprisoned for a violent crime. The information stored on the register is private; the offender is not alerted as to whether information was provided about them. Clause 17 of the Victims' Charter contains information about offenders. It refers to the ability to access the Victims Register and to receive certain information concerning the offender, such as length of sentence, likely date of release and the making of an extended supervision order.
- The victim will have the right to be informed of proceedings. Given that the police investigation stage and the court proceeding stage can be very complex and can cause confusion for a victim, the Victims' Charter ensures that the investigatory and prosecuting agencies must keep the victim informed about the investigation. Clause 8 provides that an investigatory agency, such as the police, must inform a victim about the progress of an investigation into a criminal offence. Clause 9 of the Victims' Charter states that the prosecuting agency (Director of Public Prosecutions or police prosecutor) is obliged to provide a victim with information about any charges filed against the accused person as soon as is reasonably practicable.

Note: Additional rights of the defendant that could be addressed are provided below.

- The accused will have the right to a jury. Trial by jury is based on the notion that all individuals in the community are responsible for the administration of justice. This idea dates back to the Magna Carta (1215). The *Juries Act 2000* (Vic) sets out the requirements for the composition and empanelling of juries. The Juries Commissioner is responsible for ensuring that there are enough eligible people for jury service. The names of potential jurors are selected from the electoral roll at random. The Juries Commissioner will send a questionnaire that determines eligibility to all those selected from the electoral roll.
- The accused will have the right to silence. When being questioned by a police officer, an individual does not have to respond beyond providing their name and address. In addition, at trial, the accused does not have to take the stand nor provide witnesses nor a defence. No adverse inferences can be drawn from an accused exercising their right to silence. This right is in place to ensure the accused does not incriminate himself or herself.

Mark allocation: 4 marks

- 1 mark for correctly identifying a right of the victim.
- 1 mark for correctly identifying a right of the defendant.
- 1 mark for a detailed explanation of the right of the victim.
- 1 mark for a detailed explanation of the right of the defendant.

Note: High-scoring responses must identify and explain each right in detail, with reference to relevant laws.

Question 5b

Sample response

One reason for the existence of a court hierarchy is specialisation.

Given that the courts oversee particular jurisdictions, they hear certain types of cases. As a result of hearing certain types of cases, they develop expertise in certain matters. Specifically, the personnel within courts develop expertise in the relevant laws, procedures and clientele. For example, those within the Magistrates' Court develop a thorough knowledge of summary offences, such as offensive behaviour.

In relation to the case provided, Phillip had been charged with serious assault. The County Court will have had such cases come before it previously and will be well versed in how to handle them and how to sentence the offender, with due consideration given to all relevant factors.

Mark allocation: 3 marks

- 1 mark for identifying a reason for a court hierarchy.
- 1 mark for explaining the reason for a court hierarchy.
- 1 mark for the reference to the case.

TIP

» **The VCE Legal Studies Study Design also refers to 'appeals' as a reason for a court hierarchy in determining criminal cases.**

Question 5c

Sample response

It would be entirely appropriate for the court to consider mitigating circumstances and the early guilty plea in this case. However, consideration would need to be given to other factors as well.

Mitigating circumstances are those associated with the accused that can reduce culpability and therefore the seriousness of the sanction imposed. In this case, mitigating circumstances would include Phillip's homelessness and history of drug addiction and mental health issues.

The court will also look favourably on the early guilty plea. Early guilty pleas reduce the burden on all parties and institutions, freeing up the legal system for contested matters.

However, the court would need to consider other factors that would not be looked upon favourably. These include aggravating factors, such as the serious nature of the offence, and the victim impact statement that Jill might choose to compose.

Mark allocation: 4 marks

- The response will be marked globally.
- Reference must be made to both mitigating circumstances and early guilty pleas.

Question 6a

Sample response

Two different factors that will be considered by the court when sentencing are guilty pleas and victim impact statements. Guilty pleas have many benefits. An early guilty plea will save time for the courts and community resources. In addition, the victim and the victim's family might be spared stress and uncertainty. Of course, the prosecution might accept a guilty plea to a less serious charge if there is not enough evidence to prove a more serious charge. For the offender, sentencing discounts are available for early guilty pleas.

In this case, a guilty plea will not be relevant because Minh is determined to enter a not guilty plea. However, a victim impact statement (VIS) differs from a guilty plea. With a VIS, a victim of crime is given the opportunity to make an official statement to the court on how the crime has affected his or her life. These statements will be made in court if the accused is found to be guilty. The statement can be presented in writing or orally; the victim or the prosecution can present the VIS; and the statement can refer to details such as injury, loss or damage suffered.

In this case, the use of victim impact statements will be relevant because both a young mother and an elderly man have been dramatically and negatively affected by the crime. These experiences are likely to see a harsher sentence imposed if Minh is found guilty.

Mark allocation: 4 marks

- 1 mark for defining each factor and clearly indicating that they are different by using comparative language (up to 2 marks).
- 1 mark for determining the relevance of each factor to the case (up to 2 marks).

» **The response must highlight the difference between the factors. Words such as 'whereas' and 'however' can be of benefit here.**

Question 6b

Sample response

A plea negotiation will be somewhat appropriate in this case.

Positively, a successful plea negotiation would see trial avoided. Given the matter involves multiple indictable offences, and Minh is 'adamant' she is going to plead not guilty, presumably to all charges, a trial would take many days or weeks. Avoiding trial would result in time, money and resources saved. For example, legal representation will not need to be employed for an extended period, resulting in the saving of funds for both the accused and the state. In addition, court personnel and facilities will not be required for a contested matter. Access to the criminal justice system would be enhanced.

Minh herself would benefit from a plea negotiation because entering a guilty plea to reduced charges, or a reduced number of charges, would lead to a less severe sanction. Imprisonment would still be the most likely sentence imposed, but the term to be served would be reduced. This would be advantageous for Minh as her previous term saw her unable to overcome her drug habit and it also involved a serious assault.

Further, a successful plea negotiation would aid the victims of the crime. A mother continues to seek psychological counselling and an elderly victim remains too terrified to leave the confines of his own home. If a plea negotiation was undertaken, these traumatised victims would not have to testify at trial.

However, it could be argued that a plea negotiation would be inappropriate in this matter. First, the victims may wish to testify and have their day in court, which can help a victim find closure; a successful plea negotiation would prevent this from happening.

Second, Minh might feel pressured to enter a guilty plea. This would not be fair if she is, in fact, innocent of the offences. In addition, if Minh did accept a deal, she would receive a consequence that is less severe than the one she would receive if she was to be found guilty at trial. The victims and broader society might believe such a sanction to be insufficient.

Finally, concerns are often expressed that plea negotiations unfold behind closed doors, conflicting with the principle of open justice which is fundamental to the legal system.

Mark allocation: 5 marks

- The response will be marked globally.
- Both the appropriateness and the inappropriateness of plea negotiations need to be addressed in the response.
- Full marks can only be achieved with meaningful reference to the stimulus material.

TIP

» **When you are asked to 'discuss' a topic, you must address both sides of the argument. However, you should provide greater detail for your main point than the counterpoint.**

Question 6c

Sample response

A community corrections order (CCO) can fulfil the purposes of criminal sanctions to an extent, depending on the specific offender, their capacity to adhere to any special conditions, and the appropriateness of such a sanction in the circumstances. Minh's multiple indictable offence charges are likely to be tried in the County or Supreme Court. Both of these courts are able to impose a CCO as an alternative to a fine or a term of imprisonment, if those options were deemed not appropriate. Minh would also need to agree to the order.

A CCO can serve to punish Minh as restrictions are placed on her liberty, which can help achieve the purposes of just punishment and denunciation. She must report to Corrections Victoria (CV) within two days of the order being made and meet with a supervisor regularly; she must inform CV of a change of address; and she must stay in Victoria unless permission is granted to do otherwise. A CCO can also specifically deter Minh, and generally deter the wider society, from future offending because of the requirement to undertake up to 600 hours of community service work, without pay, which is a substantial imposition on the individual. Minh has proved that she is a repeat offender so every effort must be made to deter her from recidivist behaviour. It can be argued that the CCO provides protection because the individual must not commit further offences during the order, which is necessary given the fear experienced by Minh's victims. The individual must also be required to stay away from particular individuals and places. Finally, a CCO can require the offender to attend treatment for drug and alcohol use. Hopefully, this will see the offender rehabilitated. Minh seems to suffer from drug addiction, which would necessitate such a condition.

Despite the benefits of a CCO, critics would suggest that it possesses many flaws. First, it could be suggested that it does not sufficiently punish Minh, given the arguably lenient consequences associated with such a sentence. Second, it could be argued that it would not sufficiently deter Minh or other offenders from future offending. Third, questions could be asked about the protective aspect of CCOs; while restrictions are in place, it's possible that the individual could reoffend as she would be living in the community. Finally, conservative commentators have argued that the CCO does not sufficiently denounce the offender and the actions committed, for the reasons stated above.

Mark allocation: 6 marks

- 3 marks for discussing how community corrections orders can fulfil multiple aims of criminal sanctions.
- 3 marks for discussing how community corrections orders do not always fulfil multiple aims of criminal sanctions.

TIP

- Use paragraphs when responding to questions to clearly structure and signpost your discussion for the assessor.
- Close application of the facts provided in the stimulus scenario is crucial to achieve top marks. Thorough knowledge and discussion of CCOs is not enough to ensure full marks.

Question 7a

Sample response

One factor that affects the ability of the criminal justice system to achieve the principles of justice is delays. These are caused by a number of factors that include developments in society (such as the motor car), new pieces of legislation and common law principles, and unnecessarily lengthy opening and closing statements. Fairness is one way that people are affected by delays in the legal system because witnesses may forget events or die prior to their case coming to trial. Equality can be affected; for example, when the delay causes an accused's funding to run out, leaving them without legal representation during trial. Delays can also inhibit access since justice delayed is justice denied, and delays will leave disputes festering in the community and accused people waiting in remand.

Another factor affecting the ability of the criminal justice system to achieve the principles of justice is costs. Legal representation is a necessity when at trial, but the cost of attaining and then maintaining the services of a solicitor and a barrister can be beyond the reach of many. Victoria Legal Aid and community legal centres exist to assist the accused, but both have limitations. These institutions can provide advice and guidance, but eligibility needs to be assessed for ongoing representation and it is enormously difficult to gain such help. A lack of representation stemming from high costs will result in a lack of fairness as unrepresented parties will not be familiar with the strict rules of evidence and procedure. Inequality exists when the accused finds they are arguing against the near-limitless resources of the prosecution. Again, access to justice will be denied.

Mark allocation: 4 marks

- 2 marks for outlining each factor (up to 4 marks).

Note: One or both factors must specifically refer and connect to the first piece of stimulus material.

TIP

- **The VCE Legal Studies Study Design refers to 'costs, time and cultural differences'. Any of these could be addressed in this question.**
- **You must refer to the actual principles of justice in your response.**

Question 7b

Sample response

The Supreme Court of Victoria aims to fulfil the principles of justice between 2020 and 2025 in a number of ways. Fairness, allowing all parties to participate in the legal process and ensuring proceedings are impartial and open, will be addressed by 'maintaining systems and supports to ensure the integrity of the Court and its work. Conducting ... hearings in public and making them available for viewing through technological means where appropriate ...'

Equality, regarding all similarly and viewing all to be of the same status regardless of background, will be addressed by 'ensuring ... equal protection of the law to all those before the Court, including in criminal cases ...'

Access, providing parties with the means to resolve disputes and achieve the right outcome, will be addressed by 'writing judgments that are clear, concise and easy to understand ...' and by 'treating all Court users with courtesy and respect [and by] respecting and promoting diversity ...'

Mark allocation: 6 marks

- 1 mark for identifying each principle of justice (up to 3 marks).
- 1 mark for connecting each principle with a relevant aim of the Supreme Court of Victoria (up to 3 marks).

TIP

» **Your challenge in this question is to attribute each principle of justice to the aims and initiatives of the Supreme Court.**

Question 7c

Sample response

The judge is an independent, impartial third party who presides over the trial. The judge will ensure that the accused is 'tried in person' and, if there is no legal representation, the judge might stay proceedings until 'legal assistance [is] assigned to the accused, where the interests of justice so require'. The strict rules of evidence and procedure will be upheld and the accused will be given the opportunity to 'cross-examine prosecution witnesses'. By ensuring the above, the accused's right to fairness will be upheld.

The jury is also an independent, impartial third party. Its responsibility in a criminal case is to listen to the arguments and evidence presented, consider the cases of the parties, and reach a decision. The right to a jury is a fundamental right belonging to the accused, ensuring the verdict is determined by peers of the accused, a random cross-section of society.

Legal practitioners employed by the accused will work to assist the accused in being tried without unreasonable delay. A solicitor and a barrister will also help the accused 'prepare a defence' and present that case in court. If necessary, legal representation will have the conviction and sentence reviewed by a higher court.

Mark allocation: 6 marks

- 1 mark for identifying each key figure or body (up to 3 marks).
- 1 mark for explaining how the rights of the accused are protected by each figure or body (up to 3 marks).
- Full marks cannot be gained if there is no reference to the stimulus material.

Question 8

Sample response

The case of Johnny involved multiple indictable offences. The crimes for which Johnny has been arrested and charged are murder and attempted murder, exceedingly serious offences and ones which are referred to in the *Crimes Act 1958*, the statute which contains most of Victoria's indictable offences. If Johnny intends to plead not guilty, he will experience a committal hearing in the Magistrates' Court. If the matter is to proceed to trial, Johnny will find himself in the Supreme Court (Trial Division), a state court which hears the most serious indictable matters.

Mark allocation: 3 marks

- 1 mark for correctly identifying indictable offences.
- 2 marks for providing a detailed explanation; at least two reasons as to why the matters are indictable need to be provided.

Question 9

Sample response

The presumption of innocence is protected within the criminal justice system in numerous ways.

First, the responsibility of proving the guilt of the accused rests with the prosecution; the accused does not have to establish his or her innocence in a court of law.

Second, the standard of proof is extensive; the prosecution must prove the guilt of the accused beyond reasonable doubt and, if there is any doubt as to the guilt of the accused, he or she must be acquitted.

Third, the right to silence links to the presumption of innocence. The accused does not have to respond to police questions, take the stand at trial or mount a defence. Indeed, no adverse inferences can be drawn from an accused choosing to remain silent.

Mark allocation: 3 marks

- 1 mark for each way by which the presumption of innocence is protected within the criminal justice system.

TIP

» **You could receive full marks if you only provide two ways by which the presumption of innocence is upheld within the criminal justice system. However, such a response would need to be an in-depth one.**

Question 10

Sample response

The right to silence addresses fairness as it ensures the accused will not incriminate himself or herself. An accused who does respond to questions when under pressure risks making statements that indicate guilt; therefore, the right to silence provides the accused with substantial protection. Importantly, no adverse inferences can be drawn from an accused not responding to police questions. In addition, no adverse inferences can be drawn from an accused not taking the stand during trial or not mounting a defence at trial. It is only fair that an accused who retains the right to silence is treated impartially.

Mark allocation: 3 marks

- Full marks can only be achieved if the response addresses what the right to silence hopes to achieve.

Question 11a

Sample response

In the criminal case against Frank, as in all criminal matters, the standard of proof is related to fairness. The responsibility of proving Frank's guilt rested with the prosecution. Significantly, the prosecution had to establish Frank's guilt beyond reasonable doubt. This means the prosecution required extensive and substantial evidence in order to convict Frank of the rape of Amaya. If extensive and substantial evidence is lacking in a criminal matter, and doubt exists as to the accused's guilt, the accused must be acquitted, ensuring fairness.

Mark allocation: 2 marks

- 1 mark for outlining the standard of proof in this case.
- 1 mark for linking the standard of proof to fairness in this case.

Question 11b

Sample response

In a criminal matter, there is no need for the accused to take the stand. This is because the burden of proof rests with the prosecution; the responsibility of proving guilt is that of the prosecution. The accused, Frank, did not give evidence in this matter as he possessed the presumption of innocence and the right to silence.

Mark allocation: 3 marks

- 1 mark for an explanation of the burden of proof.
- 1 mark for reference to the presumption of innocence.
- 1 mark for reference to the right to silence.

Question 11c

Sample response

In the criminal trial of Frank, the jury possessed many vital responsibilities. It was to have acted as an independent, impartial fact-finding body. In addition, the jury was to have represented a random cross-section of society. When presiding over the trial, the jury was to have listened to the arguments and evidence of the prosecution, including the three days of testimony provided by the accuser, Amaya, and the defence; it was to have considered the evidence; and, ideally, it was to have delivered a verdict. There are many advantages to having trial by jury, including the spreading of responsibility of decision-making over multiple sets of shoulders and providing trial by peers, incorporating members of society into the legal system.

However, due to a particular juror accessing information that had not been presented as evidence in court, the jury was discharged. This meant not only was the matter unresolved, but the time, money and resources that had been poured into the trial had been wasted.

Mark allocation: 5 marks

- The response will be marked globally.
- A detailed assessment of the role of the jury in the particular case is required. In analysing the role of the jury, you need to address impacts and consequences associated with the jury in this case.
- Stimulus material must be incorporated into the response.

Question 11d

Sample response

Either Victoria Legal Aid (VLA) or a community legal centre (CLC) could have assisted the victim, Amaya, in this case in a number of ways. Amaya could have consulted with either institution in order to ascertain her rights, including the right to give evidence using alternative arrangements, the right to be informed of proceedings, and the right to be informed of the offender's likely release date. Information as to giving evidence using alternative arrangements would have been particularly pertinent in this matter, given the allegations involved a sexual offence. In addition, VLA or a CLC could have provided Amaya with information about seeking a protection order in relation to Frank, such an order providing peace of mind for Amaya. Finally, VLA or a CLC could have provided Amaya with guidance on seeking compensation, possibly through the Victims of Crime Assistance Tribunal or through civil action.

Mark allocation: 4 marks

- The response will be marked globally.
- Multiple details regarding the assistance provided by VLA or a CLC need to be provided.
- Stimulus material must be incorporated into the response.

Question 12

Sample response

Cultural differences can affect fairness. An individual from a culturally different background, such as a migrant or an Indigenous Australian, might be unaware of the criminal nature of a particular act. In addition, there might be ignorance as to police powers and citizens' rights. The adversarial nature of the criminal justice system might be foreign to some, meaning a case might not have been sufficiently prepared or presented. That said, an individual from a culturally different background can receive advice through Victoria Legal Aid (VLA) or a community legal centre (CLC). Such advice can entail reference to one's rights and responsibilities within the criminal justice system.

Cultural differences can also affect equality. An individual from a different cultural background might not find themselves on the same level as the state-backed prosecution; they will likely lack the resources, understanding of the English language, and comprehension of the criminal justice system. However, if eligibility requirements are met, an individual from a different cultural background will be granted legal representation by VLA or a CLC. Such legal representation will possess experience and expertise which the accused lacks.

Finally, cultural differences can affect access. There might be ignorance of avenues for legal assistance, such as Victoria Legal Aid and community legal centres. There might be a lack of awareness of avenues of appeal. While ignorance of institutions which can provide assistance can exist, such institutions, if utilised, have the capacity to aid those of different cultures. For example, a CLC that specialises in dealing with First Nations people is the Victorian Aboriginal Legal Service

Mark allocation: 6 marks

- 2 marks for discussing fairness.
- 2 marks for discussing equality.
- 2 marks for discussing access.

Question 1

Sample response

The Victorian Civil and Administrative Tribunal (VCAT) is an appropriate body to assist John in resolving this dispute.

Note: Three arguments are to be presented. Examples of possible arguments are provided below.

- VCAT possesses the jurisdiction to resolve such disputes. VCAT consists of four divisions and each division is further divided into specialist lists. John's dispute would be heard by the Civil Claims List, part of VCAT's civil division. This list has the expertise to deal with disputes between consumers and traders.
- VCAT is an affordable dispute resolution institution. For a nominal fee (just over $70) the matter can go before VCAT for determination. Also worth noting is that legal representation is not required at VCAT, further aiding its affordability. This dispute, involving the relatively small sum of $500, is not worth court action.
- VCAT would be appropriate for this matter because disputes can be resolved relatively quickly in comparison to going to court. After filing an application, the matter goes to VCAT within weeks, and only if the matter has not been resolved by the parties themselves. The hearing itself should take less than one day.
- VCAT will provide an appropriately informal atmosphere for the resolution of this minor matter. Within a VCAT hearing, the third party is elevated and the disputing parties are expected to act respectfully. That said, there is an absence of strict rules of evidence and procedure, which decreases the burden experienced by the parties.
- VCAT is accessible. It is centrally located at 55 King St, Melbourne, but it can also sit in a number of other suburbs and regional centres. There is a lack of complexity associated with VCAT hearings; teleconferencing can be used if needed and interpreters can also be engaged.

Mark allocation: 5 marks

- The response will be marked globally.
- High-scoring responses will identify three distinct arguments in favour of using VCAT and provide substantial explanation supporting those arguments.
- Precise details relating to cost, time, informality and accessibility would be ideal.

TIP

» **Ideally, ensure that you incorporate precise details about VCAT in your response, rather than simply providing a broad discussion.**

Question 2

Sample response

One factor that Sheena might have considered when initiating civil action against Adriano was the limitation of actions. The *Limitation of Actions Act 1958* outlines that certain civil actions must be launched within distinct time frames. Most civil actions are to be launched within three years of the infringement of rights; those relating to traffic and workplace incidents need to be launched within six years; and defamation actions need to be launched within one year of the lowering of the plaintiff's reputation. If the time frame relating to Sheena's infringement has expired, she will not be able to pursue civil action.

Mark allocation: 3 marks

- 1 mark for identifying an appropriate factor.
- 2 marks for explaining what this factor entails.

TIP

» **The VCE Legal Studies Study Design refers to three factors to be considered when initiating civil action: costs, limitation of actions, and enforcement options. Any one of these could be used in the response.**

Question 3a

Sample response

One method of dispute resolution that Sarah could use to resolve the matter is mediation. Mediation is an effective method of resolving disputes for parties who are in an ongoing relationship because the aim of mediation is to maintain the relationship. Given the likelihood that work on Sarah's house still has to be completed, maintaining the relationship between Sarah and the building company will be essential. An independent and impartial third party (mediator/s) will be involved. This third party will attempt to allow each disputing party to express opinions on key issues and the desired outcome.

Mark allocation: 2 marks

- 1 mark for accurately identifying a relevant method of dispute resolution.
- 1 mark for describing the method of dispute resolution.

Note: Other details you could include in the description of mediation are: the mediator will not offer suggestions; often a whiteboard is used by the mediator to list issues and avenues to achieve settlement; ideally, a voluntary agreement will ultimately be reached; a written agreement, known as a 'deed of settlement' can be drawn up that is enforceable through the courts.

TIP

» **When responding to a question like this, there could also be a focus on conciliation or arbitration.**

Question 3b

Sample response

> The limitation of actions is a factor outlined in the *Limitation of Actions Act 1958* (Vic), which addresses time limits for civil actions. These time limits vary and are designed to allow applicants an amount of time in which they can pursue civil action. Legal proceedings must be initiated within a set time. Legislation has established that certain matters must be initiated within three years from when the injury was discovered; a six-year period applies to work injuries and transport accident injuries. Sarah will need to determine whether the time frame for launching legal action against the building company has expired.
>
> Enforcement issues is another factor that Sarah will need to consider. Enforcement issues refers to the infringed party's capacity to receive the awarded remedy if successful at trial. Sarah will need to be confident the building company has sufficient funds and/or assets to make her legal action worthwhile. If the building company lacks funds and/or assets, there will be little reason to litigate. That said, it is worth noting there are processes in place which allow courts to enforce civil remedies if the unsuccessful defendant does not comply with a court's order. These include a warrant of distress and a garnishee order.

Mark allocation: 3 marks

- 1 mark for addressing the limitation of actions.
- 1 mark for addressing enforcement issues.
- 1 mark for incorporation of stimulus material.

Note: A clear explanation of both factors is required.

Question 3c

Sample response

In this case, Sarah could pursue the building company for a number of different remedies. One remedy is damages, but this payment will only fulfil the purposes of civil remedies to an extent.

The aim of damages is to restore the injured party to the position it was in prior to the infringement of rights. This is done through the awarding of a monetary amount. Specific compensatory damages will address any financial loss suffered by Sarah as a result of the failed construction work.

General compensatory damages will be paid for non-financial loss, such as pain and suffering (e.g. psychological suffering). However, it is impossible to put an exact monetary value on this. Therefore, Sarah might not be fully restored to her previous position.

Mark allocation: 3 marks

- 1 mark for providing an evaluative statement with a contention.
- 1 mark for outlining how damages fulfil the purposes of civil remedies.
- 1 mark for outlining how damages do not fulfil the purposes of civil remedies.

Note: An injunction could also be discussed in response to this question.

TIPS

» **When addressing a question that asks you to discuss the extent of something, you must provide two distinct perspectives.**

» **You must provide a sentence addressing the extent to which you believe the remedy you identified can achieve its purpose. This requires you to explain why it will, will not, or will partially achieve its specific purpose.**

Question 4

Sample response

> One responsibility of a judge in a civil trial is to act as an independent and impartial third party, one not subjected to pressure or political influences, who will preside over the matter at hand. The judge will ensure that both parties are given equal opportunity to present their cases and that both are treated fairly. Strict rules of evidence and procedure will be applied by the judge to ensure that justice prevails.

Mark allocation: 2 marks

- 1 mark for identifying a responsibility.
- 1 mark for providing additional detail outlining the responsibility.

Note: Other responsibilities that you could address include: overseeing selection and empanelment of the jury (if a jury is used in a civil trial); providing a summary of evidence to the jury (if a jury is present); if no jury is present, considering the evidence and deciding which version of the facts is more likely on the balance of probabilities (subsequently, a verdict will be delivered); if finding for the plaintiff, determining the remedy.

TIP

» **If you provide multiple responsibilities, the first one addressed will be the one assessed. Listing multiple responsibilities, even if accurate, does not equate to successfully outlining one. Such an approach will not see a second mark awarded.**

Question 5a

Sample response

> The party that will possess the burden of proof in this case is the plaintiff, Sharon. This means that the responsibility of proving the wrongdoing of the accused rests with Sharon.
>
> The standard of proof in this matter is on the balance of probabilities. This means that Sharon must prove that it was likely that Yashiro committed a civil wrong.

Mark allocation: 3 marks

- 1 mark for outlining the party that will possess the burden of proof.
- 2 marks for explaining the standard of proof.

Question 5b

Sample response

Damages are civil remedies that involve a monetary payment to the infringed party, paid by the party deemed to be in the wrong. There are multiple types of damages. Compensatory damages, in the form of specific, general or aggravated damages, aim to restore the infringed party to the position they were in before the infringement. Nominal damages will be handed down if there has been a clear infringement of rights, but no great loss suffered. Exemplary damages have the aim of punishing the wrongdoer. Contemptuous damages will be awarded by the court if there is disdain for a trivial matter that has been brought to trial.

Injunctions are court orders. Mandatory injunctions compel, while action and restrictive injunctions prevent an action. Injunctions can be perpetual (ongoing) in nature or interlocutory (interim) in nature.

In this case, civil remedies will fulfil their purposes, but only to an extent. The aim of damages is to restore the injured party to their position prior to infringement of rights. This is done through the awarding of a monetary amount. Specific compensatory damages, which can be calculated exactly, will cover Sharon's medical costs and current loss of earnings. General compensatory damages will address pain and suffering and they will also cover loss of future earnings. Sharon could also potentially sue for exemplary damages (otherwise known as punitive damages), which, if Sharon is successful, would see a further sum awarded to her.

However, it is impossible for a monetary sum of any amount to fully restore the plaintiff to the position she was in prior to the accident. Despite the money awarded, Sharon will experience ongoing pain and discomfort for the rest of her life as a result of the negligence.

Mark allocation: 6 marks

- 2 marks for describing damages.
- 2 marks for describing injunctions.
- 2 marks for outlining whether civil remedies fulfil their purpose.

TIP

» **When describing damages and injunctions, you should include multiple precise details.**

Question 6

Sample response

> In this case, if Jo decides to pursue civil action, the burden of proof will rest with Jo.
>
> The standard of proof is the extent to which the liability of the defendant, the state, must be established. This will be on the balance of probabilities; in other words, it will need to be established that it was more likely than not that the state was in the wrong, and infringed Jo's rights while she was imprisoned.

Mark allocation: 3 marks

- 1 mark for addressing the burden of proof.
- 2 marks for addressing the standard of proof and incorporating meaningful reference to the case.

Question 7a

Sample response

In the matter of the local sporting club and a number of BIPOC (Black, Indigenous, people of colour) players, mediation will be appropriate to an extent.

Mediation is a less costly and time-consuming method of resolving disputes. While it might entail legal representation and financial outlay, it is a far more affordable process than judicial determination within a traditional courtroom. The affordability of mediation stems from its more efficient nature and the possible absence of legal representation. In addition, there is an absence of extensive pre-trial procedures with mediation, which will ideally lead to a more rapid resolution of the dispute, allowing both the players and the club to move on from the matter.

The less formal environment of mediation, with parties sitting on the same level as the independent, impartial third party, reduces the level of intimidation and is conducive to open and honest discussion. Such discussion will be aided by the lack of strict rules of evidence and procedure. Such an atmosphere could be suitable for the highly sensitive issues associated with the sporting club dispute.

Finally, mediation is not an adversarial process, meaning that if a resolution is reached, a mutually agreeable outcome will be achieved and, ideally, a compromise will be reached. In the case of the sporting club, it might acknowledge some wrongdoing, while the infringed players might accept there was no ill intent behind the club's actions.

However, there can be difficulties with mediation, meaning it is not an appropriate method on some occasions. If there is a power imbalance between the disputing parties, mediation will not be ideal. The club is a more powerful entity than the BIPOC players. The players might be intimidated and too willing to compromise.

Mediation will also not be appropriate if one or both parties desire a legally binding decision. Mediation will not automatically result in a legally binding decision and a deed of settlement will be required for an agreement to become enforceable.

Finally, mediation will not be appropriate if the disputing parties are unwilling to cooperate. For mediation to succeed in this instance, both the sporting club and the players would need to be committed to working towards a resolution.

Mark allocation: 6 marks

- 3 marks for addressing the appropriateness of mediation in this matter.
- 3 marks for addressing the inappropriateness of mediation in this matter.

Note: You do not need to provide equal weighting for each side.

Question 7b

Sample response

In the local sporting club matter, the parties might have benefited from using a court to resolve the dispute.

Taking a matter to court for a resolution has a number of advantages. First, an independent and impartial third party will preside over the civil trial. The magistrate or judge will have no connection to either party and will ensure each party has the opportunity to present its case to the court. Both the club and the players will be treated without fear or favour.

Second, strict rules of evidence and procedure apply within a courtroom. This means some types of evidence will be admissible, while other types will be inadmissible. Inadmissible evidence includes unreliable and irrelevant evidence. The rules of procedure will ensure each party has the chance to present their respective case and examine and cross-examine witnesses. The strict rules of evidence and procedure relate to fairness.

Third, a legally binding decision can be imposed. Such a decision, which would either be in favour of the club or in favour of the players, would see parties compelled to follow the outcome. If the party allegedly in the wrong – the club – was deemed liable, and did not abide by the court's finding, the remedy could be enforced through the courts.

Finally, if a party is dissatisfied with the outcome, either on a point of fact, point of law, or extent of damages, an appeal can be launched in a higher court. The appellate court will review the original outcome.

Mark allocation: 4 marks

- The response will be marked globally.
- The response must present multiple benefits of using a court to resolve the dispute.

Question 8

Sample response

A court hierarchy is needed in the civil justice system for numerous reasons.

One reason for a court hierarchy within the civil justice system is appeals. A dissatisfied party will be able to appeal to a higher court on a number of grounds, including point of law and extent of damages. For example, an appeal can be launched from the County Court to the Supreme Court (Court of Appeal) on the grounds of excessive damages.

In addition, a court hierarchy exists to allow for administrative convenience. Less complex matters are allocated to lower courts, such as the Magistrates' Court; more complex matters are allocated to higher courts, such as the Supreme Court (Trial Division). As a result of cases being addressed in courts with distinct jurisdiction and specialised personnel, efficiency is enhanced and matters are resolved in less time-consuming and more cost-effective ways.

Mark allocation: 4 marks

- 2 marks for one reason.
- 2 marks for another reason.

TIP

» **You must refer to both 'administrative convenience' and 'appeals' in the response as these are the reasons specified in the Study Design.**

Question 9a

Sample response

In the Supreme Court case involving Luc and the state fishing club, each party possessed distinct roles.

Luc was the plaintiff, his rights having been infringed when he was a youth working with the club. As the plaintiff, Luc initiated the case. In all likelihood, Luc employed legal representation to assist him. As the initiating party, one of his roles was to disclose information. Luc would be involved in particular pre-trial procedures, such as the pleadings stage and the discovery stage, which would reveal allegations and evidence to the defendant. Another role would be to present the facts of the case. At trial, Luc possessed the burden of proof; it rests with the plaintiff to prove the liability of the defendant and that liability must be established on the balance of probabilities. Arguments and evidence in support of the plaintiff's case would be presented at trial; the defendant's witnesses would be cross-examined by the plaintiff or counsel for the plaintiff.

The fishing club was the defendant in this matter. One of the defendant's roles is to engage in pre-trial procedures. The defendant will respond to the plaintiff's writ and statement of claim with a notice of appearance and statement of defence. The defendant might request certain documents, such as medical records and psychiatric reports, from the plaintiff. Another role of the defendant is participation at trial. At trial, while the defendant does not possess the burden of proof, it will put arguments to the court and witnesses; it will cross-examine the plaintiff's witnesses in an effort to highlight a lack of credibility.

Mark allocation: 6 marks

- 3 marks for addressing the plaintiff.
- 3 marks for addressing the defendant.
- Stimulus material must be addressed to gain full marks.

Question 9b

Sample response

There are many similarities between a criminal jury and a civil jury. Both types of jury act as an independent and impartial fact-finding body; they represent a random cross-section of society. Civil and criminal juries listen to the arguments and evidence presented; retire to consider what was presented; and make a decision. Finally, both types of jury apply the law to the facts and evidence presented in court.

However, there are multiple differences. A jury will always be present in a criminal trial, while it is optional in a civil trial. A criminal jury needs to determine the guilt of the accused beyond reasonable doubt, while a civil jury needs to determine the liability of the defendant on the balance of probabilities. In certain criminal matters, a unanimous verdict is required, while in all civil matters a majority verdict of five out of six can be accepted by the court. A criminal jury only plays a role in determining the verdict; in some civil matters, the jury will also assess damages as it did here, awarding Luc $3 million for pain and suffering; $2.6 million for loss of earnings; and $87 000 for medical costs.

Mark allocation: 4 marks

- 2 marks for similarities.
- 2 marks for differences.

TIP

» **The task word 'compare' requires both similarities and differences to be addressed.**

Question 9c

Sample response

For a class action to have been appropriate in this case, multiple plaintiffs would have been needed. A class action, otherwise known as a representative proceeding, requires seven or more plaintiffs. In addition, the seven or more plaintiffs need to have been infringed by a common defendant, and suffered the same, or a similar type of loss. Therefore, for a class action to have proceeded in this matter, a further six plaintiffs who had suffered at the hands of Tank, or other workers with the state fishing team, would have needed to have come forward.

Mark allocation: 4 marks

- The response will be marked globally.
- Reference to what is required for a class action, including number of plaintiffs and a common defendant, is required.

Question 9d

Sample response

> Legal practitioners are necessary in a dispute such as this one for many reasons.
>
> If a matter involves litigation, ideally the parties will have access to experience and expertise in the relevant legal area. Legal practitioners will possess understanding of the law of negligence, the area under which Luc is suing. They will be aware of what must be established in court and how the fundamental elements of the law can be proven.
>
> A civil action will involve multiple pre-trial procedures, including the pleadings stage and the discovery stage. Legal practitioners – solicitors – are much better placed to complete these requirements. Counsel for the plaintiff will be able to outline the allegations made by Luc and his expectations as to how to resolve the matter in the writ and the statement of claim. Counsel for the defendant will be able to acknowledge certain allegations and refute others, while requesting documents of significance from Luc.
>
> At trial, legal practitioners are aware of the demands of court, including the need to comply with the strict rules of evidence and procedure. Barristers possess the capacity to make opening and closing arguments and examine, cross-examine, and re-examine witnesses.

Mark allocation: 5 marks

- The response will be marked globally.
- Reference to multiple reasons as to why legal practitioners are necessary is required.
- Stimulus material must be addressed to gain full marks.

Question 10

Sample response

> Consumer Affairs Victoria (CAV) is often an appropriate body to resolve civil disputes. According to the stimulus material, CAV will be appropriate if the matter relates to a business or rental provider/ property manager; if there has been an attempt to resolve the matter; if the matter falls within CAV's jurisdiction; if the matter has not previously been before a court or tribunal; and if the matter has a reasonable chance of being resolved.
>
> However, CAV will not be appropriate if the parties are unlikely to cooperate. CAV uses the dispute resolution method of conciliation for which cooperation is vital. In addition, CAV will not be appropriate if there is a desire for the outcome to be legally binding, as such a decision cannot be made by CAV.
>
> Finally, complex matters or those involving large monetary sums might be better handled by a court using judicial determination as opposed to the relatively informal CAV.

Mark allocation: 6 marks

- 3 marks for the appropriateness of CAV.
- 3 marks for the inappropriateness of CAV.
- Stimulus material must be addressed to gain full marks.

TIP

» **Equal weighting in the discussion of appropriateness and inappropriateness is not required. You can favour one side over the other.**

Question 11

Sample response

The civil justice system provides for fairness. Alternative methods (including mediation, conciliation and arbitration) bring the parties together in a less formal environment. Each party has the opportunity to present its case, free from intimidation. Ultimately, it is hoped an outcome agreeable to both parties will be reached.

The court hierarchy allows for a dissatisfied party to appeal to a higher court in which the original decision can be reviewed by one judge or a panel of judges. Also, a range of civil remedies exist which serve to restore the infringed party to the position it was in prior to the infringement – accomplished through damages – or to rectify the situation faced by the infringed party – accomplished through injunctions.

The civil justice system also allows for equality. The presence of an independent third party – a judge or a magistrate – will ensure that both disputing parties have the opportunity to present their respective cases. In addition, if a jury is present, no juror will have any link to either of the disputing parties. Significantly, both parties to a civil action can be legally represented, meaning both parties can have their cases prepared and presented by a practitioner who has experience and expertise.

Finally, the civil justice system allows for access. The existence of a court hierarchy provides for administrative convenience. As a result of distinct cases being allocated to particular courts, efficiency is enhanced and costs and delays are minimised, enhancing the accessibility. The ability to engage in a class action also aids access. An individual, who ordinarily might not be able to pursue litigation, might be able to do so as a result of being involved in a representative proceeding. The Victorian Civil and Administrative Tribunal and Consumer Affairs Victoria exist to provide Victorians with low-cost – or no cost – dispute resolution. These institutions also strive to address matters quickly. Telecommunications links and online processes have made such institutions even more accessible.

However, the operation of the civil justice system can be hampered by costs and time. There are many costs associated with civil action. High costs stem from legal assistance and representation; court fees; jury fees if a jury is to be used; and the use of expert witnesses. Delays are also a common occurrence during a legal action, the result of extensive pre-trial procedures, a possible absence of cooperation between parties, and a lack of physical and human resources. Both costs and delays prevent the occurrence of fairness as a party might decide to abandon a civil proceeding due to the burden of it. Equality will be denied if a party has to proceed without legal representation. Access will be prevented if a party cannot afford to pursue a claim.

The civil justice system has the ability to achieve the principles of justice to a significant extent.

Mark allocation: 10 marks

- The response will be marked globally.
- There must be reference to how the civil justice system addresses each of the principles of justice.
- There must be reference to the issues of costs and time.

TIPS

» **Breaking the response up into multiple focused paragraphs is essential.**
» **Strong topic sentences at the start of each paragraph are essential.**

Question 12

Sample response

The defendant in both criminal and civil matters has the ability to access the justice system, to an extent.

In relation to criminal matters, the defendant can approach either Victoria Legal Aid (VLA) or a community legal centre (CLC) for assistance.

VLA is a government-funded body that aims to provide equal access to the legal system for all Victorians, regardless of circumstances. VLA provides free legal information and education to all Victorians. In addition, VLA provides funding for legal representation in certain circumstances. There are 15 VLA offices in Victoria. Appointments can be made to see a lawyer for free legal advice. A telephone hotline also exists, as does a website, where legal advice and information can be found. Duty lawyers are at many Victorian courts to assist people on the day of their hearing. In order to gain legal representation in a criminal matter, the accused must meet strict eligibility criteria. Consideration will be given to what the case is about, the likely benefit to the accused, the benefit to the public, and the accused's financial position.

CLCs also enhance the accessibility of the legal system. CLCs exist around Victoria to provide free legal advice and information to Victorians. They are independent bodies focusing on disadvantaged groups and people with special needs. CLCs are supported by local, state and federal government funding. Volunteers and public donations are also vital to the existence of CLCs. In relation to providing ongoing legal support, certain eligibility requirements need to be met. The accused's personal circumstances and financial position will be considered. An example of a CLC is the Central Highlands Community Legal Service.

In relation to civil matters, the defendant can attempt to have the dispute settled using alternative dispute resolution methods, such as mediation, conciliation and arbitration. These forms of dispute resolution are alternatives to the judicial determination and bring with them numerous benefits. They are generally cheaper – one reason for this being that legal representation is not required – and the process is not as lengthy.

However, there are also factors that can inhibit access to the criminal justice system. One such factor is cultural difference. Migrants and First Nations peoples can experience difficulties when they get involved with the law. For example, migrants might be unaware of legal assistance (such as duty lawyers) that is available for those who are unrepresented. An unrepresented defendant can be denied access to justice because they lack the experience and expertise required. A further example of difficulties stemming from cultural difference relates to the body language of migrants and First Nations people. Negative connotations, such as an inference of guilt, can be drawn from cultural differences in body language.

As far as the civil justice system is concerned, two factors that limit access include costs and delays. High costs stem from legal representation, expert witnesses and court fees, with total sums reaching hundreds of thousands of dollars. An aggrieved party might choose not to pursue civil action because the process is deemed unaffordable and therefore inaccessible. Delays stem from the extensive pre-trial process, lawyers' tactics and the workload of legal practitioners and courts. Delays place a burden on the legal system, creating a backlog of cases and subsequently affecting accessibility.

Note: Further elements of the criminal justice system that can be accessed by the defendant are listed below.

- Committal proceedings: these theoretically ensure that weak cases do not proceed to trial, lessening the burden on the County and Supreme Courts and freeing them up for stronger cases.
- Plea negotiations and sentence indications: both processes can result in matters being resolved efficiently. Therefore, full hearings and trials will not be needed and the system will become more successful because its workload is decreased.

Note: Further elements of the civil justice system that can be accessed by the defendant are listed below.

- The existence of the Victorian Civil and Administrative Tribunal (VCAT) and Consumer Affairs Victoria: both institutions provide affordable and informal dispute resolution in relation to particular matters.
- The use of civil pre-trial procedure: procedures such as pleadings and discovery serve to inform each party of the opposing case, encourage out-of-court settlement and, if the matter proceeds that far, reduce time and cost associated with trial.
- Case management: a more recent innovation where judges are more involved in cases from the beginning. The overseeing judge can make orders requiring certain actions and can refer parties to mediation. Case management has attempted to reduce delays, thus enhancing access.

Mark allocation: 10 marks

- The response will be marked globally.
- There must be reference to both accessibility and factors which negatively affect accessibility.

Note: There are multiple ways to approach this question in terms of structure and content.

TIP

» **The demands of the question must be acknowledged. In this instance, you must refer to both criminal and civil matters in your response and give similar consideration to both.**

Unit 4 | Area of Study 1 The people and the law-makers

Question 1

Sample response

One High Court case that had an impact on the division of constitutional law-making powers was *R v Brislan*. The Commonwealth Parliament passed the *Wireless Telegraphy Act 1905*, requiring owners of wireless sets (radios) to possess a licence. The Commonwealth believed that section 51 (v) of the Australian Constitution, focusing on 'postal, telegraphic, and other like services', enabled it to pass the law. Dulcie Williams was charged with possessing a wireless set without a licence and challenged the validity of the law, arguing that the Commonwealth did not have the power to pass it.

The High Court ruled that a wireless set was a 'like service' and that, as a result, the *Wireless Telegraphy Act 1905* was valid.

This decision was significant because it made the Commonwealth's law-making powers clear. It also developed them, increasing the power of the Commonwealth. It was now evident that the Commonwealth Parliament could make law on communication devices such as wireless sets, giving it power over the state parliaments.

Mark allocation: 4 marks

- The response will be marked globally.
- Stronger responses will involve multiple accurate and precise details associated with the case, as well as a distinct explanation as to why the case was significant in relation to the division of law-making powers.

TIP

» **Incorporate facts associated with the chosen High Court case. There must be an emphasis on the significance of the case on the division of the law-making powers.**

Question 2

Sample response

The express protection of rights acts as a check on parliament in law-making to an extent.

Within the Australian Constitution, there are five express rights which act as restrictions on the law-making power of Commonwealth Parliament. These rights include s. 51 (xxxi) – acquisition of property on just terms; s. 80 – trial by jury for indictable offences against the Commonwealth; s. 92 – freedom of movement stemming from free trade between the states; s. 116 – freedom of religion; and s. 117 – freedom from discrimination based on state of residence. The Commonwealth cannot make law which infringes upon these rights. If such a law is made, the law can be challenged in the High Court and the court can rule the law invalid.

However, the check of express protection of rights is limited. First, there is no comprehensiveness of rights within the Australian Constitution. There are only the five rights and these are scattered throughout the document. Second, if a law which clashes with an express right is not challenged in the High Court, it will remain. Third, in order to mount a High Court challenge, the initiating party will require time, money and standing. If any of these is lacking, the matter will not proceed.

Mark allocation: 6 marks

- 3 marks for how the express protection of rights acts as a check.
- 3 marks for how the express protection of rights is limited as a check.

TIPS

» **An evaluation requires both the strengths and weaknesses of the check to be addressed.**

» **However, there does not need to be an equal amount of detail on the strengths and weaknesses. The response must address the main argument established at the start of the answer.**

Question 3

Sample response

One other High Court case that had an impact on the division of law-making powers was *R v Brislan*. Section 51 (v) of the Constitution gives the Commonwealth the power to make law on 'postal, telegraphic, telephonic and other like services'. The Commonwealth Parliament passed the *Wireless Telegraphy Act 1905*, requiring all owners of wireless sets (radios) to hold a licence. Officers of the Postmaster-General's Department visited Dulcie Williams' premises and found a wireless set connected to an indoor aerial. Williams admitted that she owned the wireless and that she did not possess a licence. Dulcie Williams was charged with not holding a licence and was convicted in Sydney's Court of Petty Sessions. The matter went to the High Court for appeal where it was argued that the Commonwealth had acted beyond its powers because 'wireless sets' were not mentioned in section 51 (v). The High Court interpreted the term 'other like services' to include 'broadcasting to wireless sets'. The case changed the division of law-making powers, extending the Commonwealth's power to legislate regarding postal, telegraphic, telephonic and other like services to include broadcasting to wireless sets.

Mark allocation: 5 marks

- The response will be marked globally.
- Essential elements that should be included in the response include:
  - case title
  - facts of the case
  - issue/s of the case
  - decision of the case
  - significance of the case.

TIP

» ***R v Brislan*** **is just one example that could be used. Another case commonly studied is *Commonwealth v Tasmania 1983*, also known as the 'Tasmanian Dam Case'.**

Question 4

Sample response

The Victorian Parliament is able to make law on medicinal cannabis due to the division of law-making powers. The Australian Constitution divides law-making powers between the Commonwealth and state parliaments. Exclusive powers are those specifically outlined in the Constitution, which only the Commonwealth possesses. These powers are exclusive due to their nature – e.g. section 51 (xix) regarding naturalisation and aliens – or due to prohibitions on states outlined in other sections – e.g. section 51 (vi), which states that only the Commonwealth can make laws on defence, and states cannot raise armies or navies (section 114). There is no mention of regulation of drugs such as cannabis or medical treatment in the exclusive affairs listed in the Constitution.

The Australian Constitution also outlines concurrent powers. These are law-making powers explicitly outlined in the constitution and shared between the Commonwealth and the states. When an inconsistency arises, the Commonwealth law shall prevail and the state law, to the extent of the inconsistency, shall be invalid. There is no concurrent head of power that would be applicable to the regulation of cannabis outlined in the source material. As such, it appears to be a residual power, one of the powers that was not given to the Commonwealth at Federation, which are areas not explicitly listed in the Constitution and as such 'reside' with the states. While the Constitution does not directly mention residual power, s. 106 recognises states' constitutions and section 107 recognises states' law-making powers.

In terms of making laws on drugs, such as medicinal cannabis, the Victorian Parliament relies on its residual law-making powers. The Bill covers topics such as health and crime, which are determined to be within the legislative jurisdiction of the states and, as such, their authority to legislate is well established.

Mark allocation: 4 marks

- 1 mark for addressing each of the key terms of 'exclusive', 'concurrent' and 'residual' law-making powers (up to 3 marks).
- 1 mark for including reference to the stimulus material.

TIP

» **When dealing with questions such as these, you will not receive full marks for a response that does not reference the stimulus material.**

Question 5a

Sample response

> If the government wished to increase protection for targets of online abuse and bullying, it is likely that the Bill (the proposed law) would first be introduced into the lower house, the House of Representatives. Given the government has the majority of seats in the lower house and, because the lower house represents the wishes of the majority of Australian voters, consideration would be given to whether the proposed law reflects those people. This would take place through discussion and debate.
>
> Having passed the lower house, the Bill would proceed to the upper house, the Senate. Here the Senate would act as a house of review, considering the Bill in detail. When reviewing the law, the interests of all states and territories would be given equal consideration. Given the current composition of the Senate, the focus would be on the views of minor political parties and the people they represent.
>
> If the Bill passes both the lower house and the upper house, it will ultimately proceed to the Crown. At Commonwealth level, the Crown is represented by the Governor-General, currently Samantha Mostyn. It is the responsibility of the Governor-General to provide royal assent (formal approval) of the Bill.

Mark allocation: 6 marks

- 2 marks for each feature of Commonwealth Parliament: House of Representatives, Senate, Crown (up to 6 marks).

Note: It is crucial that the roles of the lower house, upper house, and Crown are addressed in relation to law-making.

TIP

» **With any question that requires multiple focuses, you should break your response up into multiple paragraphs.**

Question 5b

Sample response

If the state of Victoria made law that conflicted with the Commonwealth's efforts to regulate the 'online world', the validity of that state law could be questioned in the High Court. According to section 109 of the Australian Constitution, if a state law clashes with a Commonwealth law, the latter shall prevail and the former, to the extent of the inconsistency, shall be deemed invalid.

Mark allocation: 3 marks

- 1 mark for identifying that the state law could be challenged in the High Court.
- 2 marks for identifying and outlining section 109 of the Australian Constitution.

TIP

» **When addressing section 109, it is vital to address the section in full, including reference to 'to the extent of the inconsistency'.**

Question 6

Sample response

Judicial activism unquestionably affects the ability of courts to make law. Judicial activism involves judges viewing themselves as law-makers and being willing to develop law. Such judges can be described as radical. An activist approach was seen in the case of Kevin and Jennifer, which began in the Family Court and proceeded to the Full Court of the Family Court. This case focused on the validity of a marriage (before marriage equality was legalised in Australia) between Kevin, a transgender man who had undergone gender reassignment surgery, and Jennifer. It was ruled that the marriage was valid. This approach led to development in the law.

OR

Judicial conservatism unquestionably affects the ability of the courts to make law. Judicial conservatism involves judges not viewing themselves as law-makers and therefore being unwilling to develop law. Such judges can be described as being traditional in their approach. A conservative approach was seen in the Trigwell case. The case involved an antiquated precedent relating to a stock-owner not possessing a duty of care for roaming livestock and the damage caused by that roaming livestock. The majority of the High Court justices presiding over the case refused to move away from the precedent. Subsequently, it was left to the Victorian Parliament to change the law.

Mark allocation: 3 marks

- The response will be marked globally.
- Stronger responses will include a definition of the term 'judicial conservatism' or 'judicial activism' prior to an assessment of its effect on courts as law-makers. An example could be used to illustrate the point.

TIP

» **Read the question carefully. It requires discussion of only one of 'judicial conservatism' or 'judicial activism'.**

Question 7

Sample response

One factor that affects the ability of parliament to make law is the bicameral structure of parliament. Importantly, the bicameral structure of parliament contributes to the representative nature of parliament. In the case of federal parliament, the lower house represents the will of the majority of people; the upper house provides equal representation for each state or territory – or each region in Victoria. In theory, this means that a range of interests are represented in the law-making process.

However, parliament might not provide a forum for debate that reflects the public's best interests. This is because parliament is dominated by 'party politics'. In other words, Members of Parliament (MPs) might represent the views of their political parties rather than their electorates. The upper house can also prove to be an obstacle if the government does not have sufficient support in the upper house. The upper house might act to frustrate the legislative program of the government and block the passage of legislation.

Another factor that affects the ability of parliament to make law is international pressures. International pressures can stem from the United Nations, other countries, or individuals, such as activists. In recent times, there have been international pressures placed on Australia to address environmental matters in order to combat climate change. There have also been international pressures in relation to the handling of refugees. If Australia risks being a global pariah or faces further consequences on a world scale, the Commonwealth Parliament will act by passing necessary legislation.

However, if it is believed what is being demanded at a global level is contrary to Australia's interests, the parliament might not act. For example, if taking certain environmental measures will result in substantial economic ramifications, including unemployment, legislation might not be initiated.

Mark allocation: 8 marks

- 2 marks for explaining how each factor assists in law-making by parliament (up to 4 marks).
- 2 marks for explaining how each factor might hinder parliament in making law (up to 4 marks).

Question 8

Sample response

> The Senate is largely representative in law-making. Theoretically, the Senate is designed to represent the interests of the states and territories. Given that each state has 12 senators and each territory has two senators, the states have equal representation in the Senate, ensuring that those with smaller populations are acknowledged when proposed laws are being discussed. Therefore, states such as Tasmania and Western Australia are not disadvantaged. The existence of senators from a range of political parties within the Senate also allows for different views to be heard.
>
> However, it could be argued that senators are more inclined to operate in support of their distinct political parties as opposed to their states of origin, conflicting with the theoretical purpose of the Senate. This issue is compounded when a number of political parties, such as the Centre Alliance and Pauline Hanson's One Nation Party, reflect the political interests of a relatively small number of Australians. Given the composition of the Senate in 2019, the government would have required the support of multiple minor parties to pass legislation. In such instances, the government often has to engage in deals and resort to compromise to pass law, which can result in legislation not necessarily being reflective of the majority.

Mark allocation: 4 marks

- 2 marks for acknowledging that the Senate is representative in law-making.
- 2 marks for providing a counterargument.

Question 9

Sample response

Without question, judges have the capacity to make law in Australian courts, as stated by Justice Mason in 1996. However, there are factors that limit the ability of courts to make law.

Courts can make law in two ways. A court makes 'common law' when it makes a decision on a new situation for which no law exists; that is, when there is no legislation covering the area. The reasoning behind the decision (the *ratio decidendi*) becomes binding on all lower courts in the same hierarchy. Law is created and is to be followed by all lower courts in the same hierarchy. Precedent, a legal principle, is set. The rule of *stare decisis* applies to enforce what has been decided. Precedent can also be persuasive, such precedent stemming from a lower court, a court in the same level as the current court, or a court from a different hierarchy. A famous precedent was established in the British case of *Donoghue v Stevenson* (1932). There had been no law relating to negligence in England when Donoghue fell ill, having consumed a soft drink containing a decomposed snail. She sued Stevenson, the soft drink manufacturer, who was found to be in the wrong. It was ruled that manufacturers owe a duty of care to the ultimate consumer.

A court can also make law when engaging in 'statutory interpretation'. Judges interpret an Act of Parliament when there is a dispute about the intention or meaning of the words used. Interpretation is required in order to resolve the dispute. Meaning is given to terms within the statute and a precedent is created as a result. In *Deing v Tarola* (1993), the terms 'regulated weapon' and 'lawful excuse' required interpretation in the Supreme Court Trial Division when a man had been convicted of possessing a black leather belt with raised silver studs.

Despite the fact that precedent is binding, there is a degree of flexibility associated with it, providing future judges with the opportunity to develop the law. Processes include reversing, which occurs on appeal; overruling, which involves a superior court moving away from the precedent set by a lower court; distinguishing, which involves differences in material facts being identified and thus the precedent being avoided; and disapproving, whereby a court on the same level as the precedent-setting court establishes a new precedent.

However, there are factors which act as limitations on the courts. The doctrine of precedent itself can act as a limiting factor due to its binding nature. There have been instances in the past where judges have been reluctant to move away from established law. One such case was the infamous Rape in Marriage case of 1985 when a husband was acquitted of raping his wife because they were still living together. An antiquated precedent was applied.

Judicial conservatism can also act as a limiting factor. Judges who are conservative do not see themselves as law-makers but as dispute-resolvers. One instance of judicial conservatism in Australia was the Trigwell case of 1979 when the High Court upheld an antiquated precedent that farmers do not owe a duty of care for roaming livestock, freeing them of liability for damage caused.

> Costs and time associated with bringing a case to court affect the ability of courts to make law. If the costs of legal action are deemed excessive, which they often are due to the expenses of legal representation and court fees, and time demands are too great, which is often the case due to delays, a party might decide not to pursue a matter. If this occurs, the matter will not arise before the court, and a law will not be made.
>
> A similar situation exists with standing. If a party does not possess standing, meaning that the party is not more affected by a matter than a member of the general public, the case will not proceed. If the case does not proceed, law cannot be made by the court.
>
> Therefore, while courts can make law (and they have made law in many crucial areas), there are restrictions that prevent law-making on occasion.

Mark allocation: 10 marks

- The response will be marked globally.
- To achieve high marks, the response will need to acknowledge both sides of the argument, although they do not need to be discussed equally.
- A concluding statement is also expected for higher marks.

TIP

» **You need to plan your response to such an extensive question carefully.**

Question 10

Sample response

> If a court is required to interpret the phrase 'eligible patient' in the future, more explicit and detailed meaning as to what exactly constitutes an 'eligible patient' would be given, and that meaning would be established as precedent. This interpretation would be binding on courts in the future if established by a superior court, leading to consistency and predictability in the way the term 'eligible patient' is interpreted. For example, a wider group of people could be eligible to legally access cannabis for medical treatment. The precedent would be merely persuasive if the interpretation is provided by a lower court in the court hierarchy.

Mark allocation: 3 marks

- 1 mark for identifying the impact.
- 2 marks for closely linking the explanation to the specific facts provided in the source material.

Question 11a

Sample response

> One factor that affected the ability of the High Court to change the law in this case was the doctrine of precedent. As part of the doctrine of precedent, judges are to follow the legal reasoning behind the decisions of higher courts when resolving disputes. This application of past precedent helps to ensure predictability and consistency. However, difficulties associated with the doctrine of precedent can arise. As was seen with the Trigwell case, antiquated precedents can be applied, resulting in injustice.
>
> Another factor that affected the ability of the High Court to change the law in this case was judicial conservatism. Judicial conservatism refers to the idea that the courts should show restraint when making decisions and rulings that could lead to significant changes in law. Judges who adopt a conservative approach will not move far beyond the established law. The belief exists that the parliament has more authority to implement major law reform than judges, who are unelected. The traditional approach to law-making is opposite to the concept of judicial activism; the idea that judges should consider a range of social and political factors.

Mark allocation: 4 marks

- 1 mark for identifying each factor (up to 2 marks).
- 1 mark for the explanation of each factor (up to 2 marks).

Question 11b

Sample response

> The statement made is inaccurate to a degree. While parliament and the courts are separate institutions, the two bodies relate in a number of ways.
>
> In the matter of Trigwell, abrogation occurred. Abrogation occurs if a court makes a law deemed inappropriate and the parliament overrides the common law. The parliament can do this because parliament is the ultimate law-making body. This could be seen in the Parliament of Victoria's response to the Trigwell case.
>
> In addition, court decisions influence changes in the laws made by parliament. For example, in the Trigwell case, the Parliament of Victoria reacted to the judgment by passing law that stated it was more appropriate for parliament to legislate in this case.
>
> It is also important that parliament and the courts relate in other ways, too. Courts interpret laws made by parliament. Statutory interpretation involves courts giving meaning to unclear terms in legislation in order to resolve a case. Parliament can also codify decisions made by courts, incorporating precedent into legislation.

Mark allocation: 6 marks

- 1 mark for identifying each relationship between parliament and the courts (up to 3 marks).
- 1 mark for explaining the relationship identified (up to 3 marks).

Question 12

Sample response

> The Crown possesses an important role in law-making at Commonwealth level. Once a Bill has passed both the lower house, the House of Representatives, and the upper house, the Senate, it will proceed to the King's representative, the Governor-General, for royal assent. Royal assent involves formal approval being given to the Bill, allowing it to become an Act of Parliament.

Mark allocation: 2 marks

- 1 mark for reference to 'royal assent'.
- 1 mark for an explanation of what 'royal assent' entails.

TIP

» **Relatively straightforward questions, such as this one, are becoming rarer in the examination, but they are still posed on occasion. Given the greater number of higher-order thinking questions in the current examinations, you need to capitalise when lower-order thinking questions are asked by ensuring you earn all the marks available.**

Question 13

Sample response

The role of the upper house of the Parliament of Victoria is distinct from that of the lower house of the Parliament of Victoria

The upper house of the Parliament of Victoria, the Legislative Council, provides each region with equal representation. There are eight regions across Victoria and five Members of the Legislative Council (MLCs) are elected from each region, resulting in a total of 40 MLCs; this ensures both urban and rural areas are given equal consideration when laws are being made. In addition, the Legislative Council acts as a house of review. It will scrutinise Bills that have been passed by the lower house, ensuring they are just and reasonable.

The lower house, the Legislative Assembly, has different roles. While the upper house provides equal representation for the regions, the lower house represents the majority when laws are being made. There are 88 members in the Legislative Assembly, one from each of the 88 districts (also known as electorates, determined on population) in the lower house so that metropolitan areas have a substantial voice. While the upper house scrutinises government, the lower house is the base of government, the political party, or parties in coalition, with the majority of seats in the lower house. As a result of government being based in the lower house, most Bills are initiated here.

Mark allocation: 4 marks

- 2 marks for addressing the upper house.
- 2 marks for addressing the lower house.

Question 14

Sample response

The separation of the legislative, executive and judicial powers acts as a check on parliament in law-making by ensuring that no one body has complete control over the three functions of the legal system.

The legislative function, involving the making of law, belongs to parliament; the executive function, involving the administration of law, belongs to the King's representative in theory, but the cabinet in practice; and the judicial function, involving the application of the law to resolve disputes, belongs to the courts.

As a result of the three functions of the legal system being separated, a system of checks and balances exists. The laws of the parliament can be checked by the courts; if parliament has gone beyond its law-making power as granted by the Australian Constitution, the law can be ruled invalid. In addition, the actions of the government can be scrutinised by the parliament and government can be held to account.

Mark allocation: 5 marks

- The response will be marked globally.
- It will not be sufficient to merely outline the separation of powers principle. There must be reference to how the principle acts as a check on parliament in law-making.

Question 15

Sample response

The High Court has protected the principle of representative government in a number of notable cases. These cases involved the High Court interpreting s. 7 and s. 24 of the Australian Constitution and handing down some significant rulings.

The principle of representative government as outlined in s. 7 states that members of the Senate are to be elected by the people, while s. 24 states that members of the House of Representatives are to be elected by the people.

In the Political Advertising Case (1992), the High Court ruled that there is an implied right to the freedom of political communication within the Australian Constitution. The *Political Broadcasts and Political Disclosures Act 1991*, which prohibited advertising on radio and television during local, state and federal elections, was challenged in the High Court. The court deemed the law invalid as, by limiting political communication, it was preventing citizens from making an informed vote. It was held that an informed vote is fundamental to having a representative government.

In *Roach v Electoral Commissioner* (2007), the High Court ruled that there is a limited right to vote. Commonwealth law, which prohibited all prisoners from voting, was challenged in the High Court. An Indigenous female prisoner, Vicki Lee Roach, was the figurehead of the case. The High Court ruled that prohibiting all prisoners from voting was invalid, based on the principle of representative government established in s. 7 and s. 24. However, a previous prohibition on prisoners serving three or more years from voting was ruled to be acceptable.

Mark allocation: 5 marks

- The response will be marked globally.
- Reference to specific cases, and how the High Court protected the principle of representative government in those cases, will be of immense benefit.

Question 16

Sample response

> One effect of the court's interpretation of legislation in *Mansfield v Kelly* was that meaning was given to words within the *Summary Offences Act 1966*. Specifically, it was ruled that a 'public place' included being in a private car parked on a public street.
>
> Another effect of the court's interpretation of legislation in *Mansfield v Kelly* was that the scope of the law was broadened, as opposed to being narrowed. Instead of acquitting the defendant due to them being in a private car, the defendant was deemed guilty because 'public place' included being in a private car on a public street.

Mark allocation: 4 marks

- 2 marks for outlining one effect; the effect is to be identified with subsequent detail provided.
- 2 marks for outlining another effect; the effect is to be identified with subsequent detail provided.

Question 1

Sample response

Royal commissions can play a major role in law reform, placing the onus on parliament to respond to recommendations made. A royal commission will be established by the King's representative, on the advice of the government of the day, in response to a matter of major concern. This was the case when the Royal Commission into the Management of Police Informants was established, following revelations that criminal lawyer Nicola Gobbo was acting as a police informer. Once established, the royal commission will investigate the area of concern. Its processes will include receiving submissions from affected individuals and bodies, and conducting private and public hearings. Once its investigations are completed, the royal commission will compile its recommendations for law reform into a report. There were 111 recommendations, directed towards the Victorian Government and Victoria Police, made in regard to the Lawyer X matter. It is then up to the relevant bodies as to whether reform will be implemented. That said, given the regard in which royal commissions are held and the extent of their investigations, parliament tends to act on the recommendations made.

OR

Parliamentary committees can play a major role in law reform, placing the onus on parliament to respond to recommendations made. In recent times, the Integrity and Oversight Committee was established as a result of two previous committees being amalgamated. Committees are formed by members of one or both houses and conduct inquiries into particular issues. Terms of reference will dictate what a committee will investigate. The committees will request input from the broader community, and affected individuals and groups can make submissions. In this way, recommendations made by parliamentary committees will reflect society's values and wishes.

Mark allocation: 4 marks

- The response will be marked globally.
- The actions of a royal commission or a parliamentary committee must be addressed in the response.
- Stimulus material must be incorporated into the response.

Question 2a

Sample response

> The Royal Commission into Family Violence was restricted from influencing a change in the law by its terms of reference and its aims. A royal commission must operate within its terms of reference and it cannot go beyond them. In this instance, the royal commission aimed to make recommendations that would 'foster a violence-free society', 'reduce and aim to eliminate family violence' and 'prevent the occurrence and escalation of family violence'. While the royal commission might make recommendations in an attempt to fulfil its aims, there is no guarantee that the government of the day will legislate based on the recommendations.

OR

> The terms of reference and aims of the Inquiry into Drug Law Reform restrict the parliamentary committee from influencing change in the law. Specifically, the inquiry is to assess the 'effectiveness of laws, procedures and regulations relating to illicit and synthetic drugs' and the 'practice of other Australian states and territories', as well as 'overseas jurisdictions and their approach'. The inquiry is expected to abide by these terms of reference when investigating the law and considering possible reform. Thus, the committee is restricted in what it can consider.

Mark allocation: 3 marks

- 1 mark for acknowledging that the royal commission / parliamentary committee was restricted.
- 1 mark for explaining how it was restricted.
- 1 mark for reference to the stimulus material.

Question 2b

Sample response

Individuals can influence law reform to a significant extent.

One source reveals that there had been an 'unprecedented investment of $572 million' by the Victorian government in an attempt to introduce reforms and to 'start implementing the most urgent recommendations'. This suggests that the voices of many of those who gave evidence at the royal commission have been heeded and legislative action has stemmed from the testimony and findings.

However, there is no guarantee that a royal commission will make recommendations in line with the beliefs of certain individuals. In addition, there is no guarantee that parliament will respond to the findings of a royal commission.

Individuals can also use petitions and demonstrations in an attempt to influence change in law. Petitions are formal, written requests for change accompanied by at least one signature. This is a peaceful, respectful way by which to communicate demands. Petitions are tabled in parliament and can illustrate the demands of a large group. That said, it is unlikely that reform will occur if the petition only contains a small number of signatures or if the matter pertains to a controversial area.

Demonstrations involve individuals and groups of like-minded people publicly gathering to put forward their demands. A demonstration can be effective because it can attract attention to a particular cause, especially if there is media coverage.

Despite this, a demonstration can be ineffective if it is disruptive or if it involves criminal behaviour. An example of an ineffective demonstration was the one recently held in Flagstaff Gardens in Melbourne, with those involved using marijuana in an effort to have the drug decriminalised.

Individuals can influence the law in a number of ways, but the effectiveness of the methods adopted will vary based on different circumstances.

Mark allocation: 6 marks

- 2 marks for each method explained, including one positive aspect and one negative aspect for each (up to 4 marks).
- 2 marks for an overall evaluative comment.

Note: This response discusses both petitions and demonstrations in detail, but only one is required to attain full marks.

Question 2c

Sample response

Royal commissions and parliamentary committees can influence law reform, but the Victorian Law Reform Commission (VLRC) also plays a vital role.

The VLRC, established in 2001, is a government-funded formal law reform body. It aims to be independent in its operation, inclusive in its investigation and innovative in its recommendations. Each of these aims is admirable, ensuring fair, just and contemporary recommendations.

The VLRC monitors and coordinates law reform activity in Victoria. It generally operates upon receiving a reference from the Attorney-General, but it can investigate minor matters without such reference. It also operates to educate the public about law reform.

The VLRC uses a number of processes when investigating possible changes to the law. One such process is receiving submissions from interested members of the public, pressure groups and experts. The VLRC invites submissions in order to be more informed about the views of society on the issue at hand. Another process used by the VLRC is that of holding forums and roundtable discussions. This is a further attempt by the VLRC to ascertain the views of society, determine the viability of a new law and to decide what the new law should constitute.

For example, the VLRC investigated the issue of medicinal cannabis. The matter was referred to the VLRC by the Attorney-General in 2014. Subsequently, an issues paper was released, submissions were called for (99 submissions were received in total), public consultations were held and a report was tabled in the Parliament of Victoria in October 2015. The Parliament of Victoria accepted the recommendations made in the report and ultimately legislation was passed allowing the use of medicinal cannabis in certain situations. In this instance, there was obvious need for reform and a requirement for a move away from traditional values and approaches.

The VLRC has played a major role in influencing legislative change over many years and for good reason.

Mark allocation: 8 marks

- The response will be marked globally.
- Stronger responses will provide an explanation of what the VLRC does, and the methods and processes it employs, and include an example. Evaluative comments are to be made throughout.

TIP

» **In your response, you could include reference to the VLRC's background, its processes, its strengths, and an example of a VLRC inquiry.**

Question 3a

Sample response

One reason for law reform is changing community values. Given parliament's representative nature, it must address the changing values of the majority of society. For example, historically there was societal disapproval of divorce, which was reflected in the *Matrimonial Causes Act 1959* (Cth). Gradually, there was a demand for more accessible divorce. As a result, the *Family Law Act 1975* (Cth) was established. The *Access to Medicinal Cannabis Act 2016* (Vic) passed the Victorian Parliament, enabling access to medicinal cannabis to defined groups of patients. The majority of people desired such a change to assist those in need.

Mark allocation: 2 marks

- 1 mark for identifying the reason for change to the law.
- 1 mark for the explanation with reference to the sources.

TIP

» **Other reasons for change to laws could be used in this response, including changes in technology, scientific research, and understanding of the impact of cannabis for certain medical conditions.**

Question 3b

Sample response

The Victorian Law Reform Commission (VLRC) undoubtedly has the ability to influence change in the law.

The influence of the VLRC was clear in relation to the area of medicinal cannabis. Given that the state government asked the VLRC to investigate the need for change to the law in specific areas, the government was more likely to act on the VLRC's recommendations. In this instance, the Attorney-General tasked the VLRC with the job of investigating medicinal cannabis in December 2014. After the VLRC's investigation, a law was passed in 2016.

Importantly, the VLRC can determine community views by holding consultations and receiving public submissions. When investigating the issue of medicinal cannabis, the VLRC held nine public consultations in metropolitan and regional Victoria, and 99 submissions were received. Given that the VLRC investigation is comprehensive, subsequent law reform can cover a whole issue. For example, the *Access to Medicinal Cannabis Act 2016* is a thorough piece of legislation.

That said, the VLRC does have some weaknesses. Parliament is not obliged to support or introduce law reform even where recommended as a result of the VLRC inquiry. In addition, parliament might accept some recommendations but reject others. It is not clear in this instance whether the government did reject implementing some recommendations.

While in this case the VLRC did play a significant role in influencing reform to access to medicinal cannabis, such influence is not always evident.

Mark allocation: 4 marks

- 1 mark for providing an overall evaluative statement with a contention.
- 3 marks for addressing the VLRC's ability to influence law reform, including reference to difficulties and obstacles relating to the VLRC's ability to influence law reform.

Question 4a

Sample response

> One reason why there is a need for change in the law is changes in technology. As technology advances, the law must adapt. This adaptation might be required to regulate the behaviour of people or companies, to provide the protection of people or companies, or both. In the source material from the National Party of Australia, it is made clear that technological developments have brought 'new threats and challenges' and, as a result, 'the online world should not be an ungoverned space'. Users of technology need to be protected when online; 'targets of online abuse and bullying should not be forced offline'.

Mark allocation: 3 marks

- 1 mark for identifying the reason for change to the law.
- 2 marks for use of the stimulus material.

Question 4b

Sample response

One effective method for individuals to influence law-makers when it comes to regulating the digital world and online activity is using petitions. A petition is a formal written request to government for action. It includes a collection of signatures gathered from supporters, although one signature is enough for it to be accepted. Significantly, a petition can be viewed as a respectful means of influencing change. The document is composed, handed to a Member of Parliament, and presented to the relevant house of parliament. In addition, at the federal level (the parliamentary level that the source refers to) a standing committee on petitions has been established to ensure that all petitions presented to the House of Representatives are considered. The committee will contact the person who initiated the petition to inform them of the response made on behalf of the house. In general, petitions illustrate substantial support for change, particularly if multiple signatures have been gathered, which is important given parliament is a representative body. Many parliaments across Australia now accept a new innovation, the e-petition (a petition signed online). Crucially, as an e-petition allows for many more supporters to be rapidly gathered, efficiency is enhanced.

Another effective method to influence law-makers is through a demonstration. This involves a gathering of like-minded individuals and groups. Vitally, when the numbers are large enough, there is a strong chance that a demonstration will bring an issue to the attention of the community and law-makers because the media is more likely to report on it. Media backing is essential as those in favour of change are likely to gain wide support for their cause. Given this, parent groups and advocates for young people in particular could embrace demonstrations as a method to influence change.

Mark allocation: 6 marks

- 3 marks for the arguments in support of each method (up to 6 marks)

Note: At least two arguments in support of each method are needed.

TIP

» **The VCE Legal Studies Study Design refers to 'petitions, demonstrations and the use of the courts', as well as the 'role of the media, including social media, in law reform'. You could address any of these methods in your response.**

Question 5

Sample response

Media, including social media, can play a major role in law reform.

Traditional forms of media, including newspapers, television and radio, can be highly influential when it comes to law reform. Newspapers contain editorials, opinion pieces, feature articles and letters to the editor; television features current affairs programs and investigative journalism shows; radio often uses talkback segments. An example of traditional media influencing law reform was seen in late 2023, when lawyer Frances Galbally penned an opinion piece in the *Herald Sun* critical of the Andrews government, accusing it of being soft on crime. Particular reference was made to the establishment of safe injecting rooms and the move to increase the age of criminal responsibility. These traditional forms of media can raise awareness among the public and simultaneously place pressure on law-makers. However, a growing section of society does not embrace traditional media, so its effectiveness as a tool to influence reform might be waning.

Social media can also be influential when it comes to law reform. Platforms such as Facebook and X (previously Twitter) allow a range of people to air their views on particular matters. Some years ago, activist group GetUp! effectively utilised YouTube to push for marriage equality. Using social media to influence law-makers is advantageous in that it is accessible, affordable, and can reach a vast number of people. However, if the individual or group using the social media platform is advocating for controversial change, law reform is unlikely as governments are wary of alienating other groups of voters.

Mark allocation: 4 marks

- The response will be marked globally.
- An analysis requires a detailed discussion of the issue.
- Both traditional forms of media and social media need to be addressed.
- At least two examples of the use of media to influence law reform need to be included.

Question 6

Sample response

The Victorian Law Reform Commission (VLRC) possesses the capacity to influence change in the law, although it is not without its weaknesses.

The VLRC investigates major areas requiring change upon receiving terms of reference from the Attorney-General. It can also investigate minor areas without reference. Upon completion of its investigation, the VLRC will publish a report containing recommendations that will be put before parliament for consideration.

Also helping the VLRC's capacity to influence law reform is its extensive process. Actions undertaken include publishing an issues paper to inform the community about work in a particular area; expert consultation; and receiving submissions from affected and interested individuals and groups. Therefore, recommendations are based on substantial research.

Recently, substantial research was undertaken when the VLRC looked into the issue of committal hearings within the criminal justice system. After a thorough investigation, the VLRC recommended the abolition of committal hearings. Their research involved submissions from bodies such as the Magistrates' Court, Victoria Legal Aid, and the Victorian Aboriginal Legal Service, which were supportive of maintaining committals, and from bodies such as the Supreme Court and Victoria Police, which were in favour of their abolition.

In the past, many VLRC recommendations were accepted and addressed in legislation by state parliament. At one point, 70% of VLRC recommendations had been acted upon.

However, the VLRC does face limitations in influencing law reform. First, the VLRC is restricted in what it can investigate. As stated previously, it requires terms of reference from the Attorney-General to look into major areas; therefore, it lacks a degree of autonomy.

Second, the VLRC's investigations can be enormously time-consuming. Years might elapse between the initiation of an inquiry and the passing of an Act of Parliament in response to VLRC recommendations. The investigation into committals took just under two years from the time the investigation began to when the report was tabled in parliament.

Third, the parliament is not obligated to accept the VLRC's recommendations. This was seen with the VLRC's investigation into committals. While the Victorian Government declared it was committed to a more efficient legal system, it is yet to act on the proposals.

Mark allocation: 8 marks

- 3 marks for addressing the ability of the VLRC to influence change.
- 3 marks for addressing limitations in relation to the VLRC.
- 2 marks for addressing a recent example and referring to the civil or criminal justice system.

Question 7

Sample response

One reason for constitutional reform is to recognise First Nations peoples. In the 1890s, when the Australian Constitution was drafted, no consideration was given to Indigenous Australians due to their perceived biological, cultural and political inferiority; the Australian Constitution was a product of its time. As the years progressed, attitudes changed and constitutional reform was deemed necessary. Indeed, in 1967, a referendum was held to give the Commonwealth Parliament the power to make law on First Nations peoples, a power previously denied by s. 51 (xxvi). This enabled the Commonwealth Parliament to pass the *Native Title Act 1993*. In addition, the referendum addressed s. 127; up to that point, First Nations peoples were not to be included in the census of the Australian population and there was a desire to alter this exclusion. The 1967 referendum was enormously successful. More recently, in 2023, there was a referendum to establish an Indigenous Voice to Parliament. This was a further attempt to combat Aboriginal disadvantages in modern society. Unlike the 1967 referendum, neither the majority of Australian voters nor the majority of voters in the majority of states supported this change.

Mark allocation: 3 marks

- 1 mark for identifying a reason for constitutional reform.
- 2 marks for the subsequent explanation.

TIP

» **Other reasons for constitutional change that could be addressed include (but are not limited to) increasing protection of rights; changing the Commonwealth's law-making powers; and reforming Australia's political system.**

Question 8

Sample response

The written words of the Australian Constitution can only be changed through a successful referendum process; this was seen in 1967.

In order to change the written words of the Australian Constitution, a constitutional amendment Bill needs to be passed by both houses of Commonwealth Parliament. An example of such a Bill was the Constitution Alteration (Aboriginals) Bill 1967. The Bill can pass one house twice and still be submitted to the voters of Australia. The proposal must be put to the voters of Australia between two and six months after the Bill's passing, during which time arguments for and against the referendum will be put to the voting population. For a successful vote, a double majority must be achieved; the majority of voters must support the change and the majority of voters in the majority of states must support the change. If the double majority is achieved, the proposal will proceed to the Governor-General for royal assent.

The 1967 referendum on Aboriginal affairs was an exceedingly successful referendum. The majority of voters backed the change, with over 90% voting in favour, and the majority of voters in the majority of states supporting the change, with all six states in favour. Subsequently, the Commonwealth Parliament gained the power to make law on First Nations peoples through alteration to s. 51 (xxvi) and First Nations peoples were to be counted in the census through the removal of s. 127.

Mark allocation: 6 marks

- 4 marks for an explanation of how the written words of the Australian Constitution can be changed.
- 2 marks for reference to the 1967 referendum.

Question 9

Sample response

One reason why a referendum might fail is Australia's conservative nature. Historically, the Australian people have been reluctant to embrace change and, particularly, constitutional change. Out of 45 referendum proposals, only eight have achieved the double majority. These successful proposals have tended to be less controversial.

Another reason why a referendum might fail is a lack of bipartisan support. In the past, if there has been a lack of support for the constitutional change from both major political parties, a significant proportion of the Australian population has been unwilling to support change. This political division was seen in the lead-up to the 2023 referendum on the Indigenous Voice to Parliament.

Mark allocation: 4 marks

- 1 mark for each reason (up to 2 marks)
- 1 mark for each explanation (up to 2 marks)

Question 10

Sample response

Both parliament and the courts possess the capacity to address calls for change to a significant extent, even though each institution faces some restrictions.

Admittedly, parliament does have certain weaknesses that limit its ability to respond to demands for change. One of them is the fact that it sits for only two-thirds of the year, maybe less. Other weaknesses are that the parliamentary process can be time-consuming and Members of Parliament (MPs) can be overly influence by pressure groups. In addition, MPs might avoid legislating as a result of the desires of a minority. Significantly, parliament might be unwilling to change the law if society is divided on an issue, as was historically the case with abortion.

However, parliament has many strengths that enhance its ability to respond to demands for change. Parliament is the ultimate law-maker and law-making is its primary role. It is an elected body that represents the will of the people; for example, when there was a desire among Victorians for harsher laws relating to the malicious online distribution of intimate images without consent, parliament responded in 2014.

Parliament's other strengths include publicly airing issues to provide a platform for debate and welcoming opposing views. MPs have regular contact with the public so they understand the needs of society; law can in turn be changed as the need arises. Indeed, law might need to change due to shifting community values. If the values of the majority change, the law must change. In recent times, the majority of Victorian society viewed the decriminalisation of cannabis for medicinal purposes to be acceptable. Subsequently, the Parliament of Victoria changed the law.

Parliament can act quickly and can determine the views of the community through the Victorian Law Reform Commission, parliamentary committees and royal commissions.

Due to parliament's representative nature, there are many ways by which individuals can influence law reform, and these methods can be impactful. One such method is the use of a petition, which is a formal written request to government for action in relation to a particular law. It includes a collection of signatures gathered from supporters, and one signature is enough for it to be accepted. For example, the petition supporting a 'Medically Supervised Injection Centre' in Victoria was published in the *Herald Sun* on 9 February 2017. Another method that can be used by individuals is a demonstration, which is a gathering of like-minded individuals and groups. Its aim is to alert the government to an issue. For example, the Free Cannabis Community organised demonstrations at Flagstaff gardens in November 2016.

Finally, different forms of media, including social media, can be used to form and reflect public opinion. Individuals will often attempt to generate media coverage when they want a law changed. In addition to traditional forms of media (newspapers, radio and television), social media platforms such as X (previously Twitter) and Facebook have become increasingly popular. In relation to the issue of marriage equality, the activist group GetUp! placed an emotional clip on YouTube promoting same-sex marriage, while Facebook allowed users to place a rainbow filter over profile pictures.

It is easy to track the impact certain posts have because there are likes, shares and comments. If politicians see certain trends, they may adjust their political stance.

Courts also have certain weaknesses that act as restrictions when addressing the need for change. The primary role of courts is to resolve disputes, so they do not necessarily have the resources required to effectively change the law. Courts cannot change the law unless a case is brought before them because a person must have legal standing, be directly affected by the issue, and be prepared to spend the time and money involved in taking a matter to court. Courts tend to be conservative and reluctant to change the law, and they may be bound by an old precedent that can lead to unjust results, as seen in the Rape in Marriage case of 1985.

That said, courts do have many strengths that enable them to respond to demands for change. Importantly, an issue cannot be deferred; it must be dealt with when it arises. Courts are free from political pressure, so they can make decisions and laws without fear of voter backlash (e.g. the 1969 Menhennitt ruling on abortion in Victoria). Also, courts can keep the law from becoming too rigid by distinguishing, overruling, reversing and disapproving previous decisions.

Mark allocation: 10 marks

- 2 marks for providing an evaluative statement addressing the ability of parliament and courts to respond to the need for law reform.
- 8 marks for addressing the ability of parliament and the courts to respond to the demands for law reform in detail. In this discussion, there must be reference to the means that individuals can use to influence change in the law.
- There must also be reference to one reason why law needs to change.

Note: A number of different structures could be used to respond to the question; the mark allocation breakdown above represents one example.

TIPS

- **It is important to note the level of precise detail in the sample responses. A detailed discussion requires multiple points to be made for both ways the courts and parliament can influence reform, and ways they are limited in doing so.**
- **You should include examples that illustrate your points wherever possible. You do not need to go into a lot of detail when using examples, but make sure the assessor can clearly understand what you are referring to (e.g. the name of a case, a piece of legislation or a brief description of a case study of law reform).**